God's Word for All Nations

Herald Press
Meditation Books

GOD'S WORD FOR ALL NATIONS

A Bible Reading Plan

J. Delbert Erb

Herald
Press

Scottdale, Pennsylvania
Waterloo, Ontario

Library of Congress Cataloging-in-Publication Data
Erb, J. Delbert (John Delbert), 1930-
  God's Word for all nations : a Bible reading plan /
J. Delbert Erb.
     p. cm.
  Includes index.
  ISBN 0-8361-9078-5 (alk. paper)
  1. Bible—Reading. 2. Devotional calendars.   I. Title.
BS617.E72 1997
220'.071—dc21   97-24494

GOD'S WORD FOR ALL NATIONS
Copyright © 1997 by Herald Press, Scottdale, Pa. 15683
    Published simultaneously in Canada by Herald Press,
    Waterloo, Ont. N2L 6H7. All rights reserved
Library of Congress Catalog Number: 97-24494
International Standard Book Number: 0-8361-9078-5
Printed in the United States of America
Book and cover design by Gwen M. Stamm

07 06 05 04 03 02 01 00 99 98 10 9 8 7 6 5 4 3 2 1

To my parents, Paul and Alta,
who encouraged me
to read the Bible

Contents

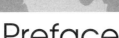

Preface

M<small>ANY</small> people wish to read through the Bible but find it difficult to do so. This plan was born out of years of Bible study and teaching.

As much as possible in this plan, the text is read in the order of the Bible story. Parallel historical accounts are grouped together. The prophets, the epistles, and many of the psalms are read in their historical contexts.

I hope this will make the biblical narrative come alive and make reading through the Bible a joyful and instructive experience. Here are several key features of this Bible-reading plan:

• The Bible is divided into 365 readings, one for each day of the year. The reader can begin at any time of the year and may change the order as desired.

• This plan can be used with any version or translation of the Scriptures.

• The days have about the same length of total readings.

• For each day a prayer and a proverb or other choice saying are supplied, matched to the readings.

• Parallel historical texts in both Old and New Testaments are listed together.

• As nearly as possible, prophetic writings are paired with their historical contexts. A few are used with New Testament texts.

• Some psalms are also paired with their historical contexts, whereas others are related to the theme of the day's reading.

• Most New Testament epistles are read in their historical contexts, but some are used as parallel readings with Old Testament texts (thus Hebrews with Leviticus).

• Undated material is sometimes grouped together or added to other readings according to subject matter.

• The compiler of this plan leaves open the questions of when biblical texts were written. Instead, he has sought to place material in a chronological order of the events about which the text speaks.

• The book of Job is placed after Genesis because it seems to have a patriarchal setting. We do not know the date of this story. We are also uncertain about the time periods of several prophets.

• I recommend that the reader glance over the references for a day before beginning to read. The selections may be from different parts of the Bible.

• The proverbs and other texts printed in this book are from the New Revised Standard Version unless otherwise identified.

• To save space, the name of a book of the Bible is sometimes abbreviated to its first letters.

As you read your Bible and meditate and pray, I wish you God's blessings and true fellowship with believers everywhere.

—*J. Delbert Erb*

Day 1

The wonder of God's Creation

1. The first account of the Creation. *Genesis 1:1—2:3*
2. Praise for God's Creation. *Psalm 104:1-35*
3. The Creation itself praises God. *Psalm 148:1-14*
4. By faith we believe it. *Hebrews 11:3*

A proverb: The Lord by wisdom founded the earth; by understanding he established the heavens; by his knowledge the deeps broke open, and the clouds drop down the dew. *Proverbs 3:19-20*

A prayer: We praise you, God, for your wonderful Creation and for your spirit of wisdom, might, and power that made our universe.

Day 2

Our response for the way the Lord created us

1. The second account of the Creation. *Genesis 2:4-25*
2. The place of man in God's Creation. *Psalm 8:1-9*
3. The attributes of the Creator. *Psalm 139:1-24*
4. The Lord of Creation. *Psalm 93:1-5*
5. The goodness and care of God. *Psalm 65:1-13*
6. God's power and strength. *Isaiah 40:12-26*

A proverb: The hearing ear and the seeing eye—the Lord has made them both. *Proverbs 20:12*

A prayer: Thank you, God, for your continual presence in Creation. Help us be good stewards of the world you have given us.

Day 3

The sin of Eve and Adam
1. The disobedience of Eve and Adam. *Genesis 3:1-24*
2. The mortality of humans. *Job 14:1-22*
3. The wrath of God against all sin. *Romans 1:18-32*
4. The evil of the foolish. *Psalm 14:1-7; 53:1-6*

A proverb: There is a way that seems to be right, but in the end it is the way to death. *Proverbs 16:25*

A prayer: Lord, forgive us for our disobedience and our foolish actions. Give us wisdom and understanding of your will that we may be faithful to you.

Day 4

The first family and the beginning of violence
1. Cain kills Abel. *Genesis 4:1-16*
2. Descendants of Adam and Eve. *Genesis 4:17—5:32; 1 Chronicles 1:1-4*
3. The faith of Abel and Enoch. *Hebrews 11:4-6*
4. The arrogance of the wicked. *Psalm 10:1-18*
5. A warning against violence. *Proverbs 1:8-19*

A proverb: The violent entice their neighbors, and lead them in a way that is not good. *Proverbs 16:29*

A prayer: O Lord, forgive us for our violent ways. Lead us in your path of love, peace, and understanding. Bless our families.

Day 5

Noah and the Flood

1. Corruption and violence. *Genesis 6:1-12*
2. God's instructions to Noah. *Genesis 6:13-22*
3. The Flood. *Genesis 7:1—8:22*
4. God's covenant with Noah. *Genesis 9:1-17*
5. The faith of Noah. *Hebrews 11:7*

A proverb: The highway of the upright avoids evil; those who guard their way preserve their lives. *Proverbs 16:17*

A prayer: Help us, God, to take your promises at their face value without doubting your Word. Thank you for your revelation to us.

Day 6

The descendants of Noah. The Tower at Babel

1. Sons of Noah. *Genesis 9:18-29*
2. Clans of Noah's sons. *Genesis 10:1-32; 1 Chronicles 1:5-27*
3. Descendants of Shem. *Genesis 11:10-26*
4. The Tower of Babel. *Genesis 11:1-9*
5. A prayer of David. *Psalm 86:1-17*

A proverb: Sheol and Abaddon are never satisfied, and human eyes are never satisfied. *Proverbs 27:20*

A prayer: Teach us your way, O Lord, that we may know your mercy, your love, and your salvation to all generations.

Day 7

God's call to Abram. His migration to Canaan

1. The family of Terah. *Genesis 11:27-32*
2. Abram obeys God's call to go to Canaan. *Genesis 12:1-9*
3. Abram and Sarai in Egypt. *Genesis 12:10-20*
4. Separation of Abram and Lot. *Genesis 13:1-18*
5. Abram rescues Lot. *Genesis 14:1-24*
6. The priest Melchizedek. *Hebrews 7:1-10*
7. The faith of Abram. *Hebrews 11:8-10*

A proverb: A generous person will be enriched, and one who gives water will get water. *Proverbs 11:25*

A prayer: Give us faith to follow you, O God, like Abram did even though we do not know the future.

Day 8

God's covenant with Abram; circumcision

1. God's promise; the covenant sealed. *Genesis 15:1-21*
2. The birth of Ishmael. *Genesis 16:1-16*
3. The covenant and circumcision. *Genesis 17:1-27*
4. Circumcision, Abraham, and justification by faith. *Romans 4:1-25*

A proverb: In the path of righteousness there is life, in walking its path there is no death. *Proverbs 12:28*

A prayer: Thank you, God, for crediting to us righteousness because of our faith in Jesus our Lord. Guide us that we may walk and live in that faith.

Day 9

The destruction of Sodom and Gomorrah

1. The three visitors to Abraham. *Genesis 18:1-15*
2. Abraham pleads for Sodom. *Genesis 18:16:33*
3. Sodom and Gomorrah destroyed. *Genesis 19:1-29*
4. The children of Lot's daughters. *Genesis 19:30-38*
5. David asks for vengeance on the wicked. *Psalm 58:1-11*

A proverb: The bloodthirsty hate the blameless, and they seek the life of the upright. *Proverbs 29:10*

A prayer: We trust in you, O God, to bring justice against all evildoers. Help us be instruments of salvation and blessing to all people.

Day 10

God blesses, tests Abraham. Abimelech. Isaac

1. Abraham and Abimelech. *Genesis 20:1-18*
2. The birth of Isaac. *Genesis 21:1-7*
3. Hagar and Ishmael sent away. *Genesis 21:8-21*
4. The treaty with Abimelech. *Genesis 21:22-34*
5. God tests Abraham's faith. *Genesis 22:1-24*
6. The faith of Sarah and Abraham. *Hebrews 11:11-19*

A proverb: The fear of the Lord is life indeed; filled with it one rests secure and suffers no harm. *Proverbs 19:23*

A prayer: Thank you, Lord, for testing our faith. Help us to understand your purpose for our lives.

Day 11

Death of Sarah. Marriage of Isaac and Rebekah
1. The death and burial of Sarah. *Genesis 23:1-20*
2. Abraham obtains a wife for Isaac. *Genesis 24:1-67*

A proverb: He who finds a wife finds a good thing, and obtains favor from the Lord. *Proverbs 18:22*

A prayer: Thank you, Lord, for directing in so many details in our lives. Help us see and follow your leading, especially in times of life-cycle changes.

Day 12

Abraham, Isaac, Ishmael, Esau, Jacob, and Abimelech
1. The death of Abraham. *Genesis 25:1-11*
2. The descendants of Ishmael. *Genesis 25:12-18*
3. Offspring of Hagar, Keturah, Sarah. *1 Chronicles 1:28-34*
4. The birth of Jacob and Esau. *Genesis 25:19-34*
5. Treaty between Isaac and Abimelech. *Genesis 26:1-33*
6. A delightful inheritance. *Psalm 16:1-11*

A proverb: In the fear of the Lord one has strong confidence, and one's children will have a refuge. *Proverbs 14:26*

A prayer: Thank you, Lord, for the inheritance you have given us. May we be faithful stewards of your blessings.

Day 13

Jacob deceives Isaac and flees to Haran

1. Esau's wives. *Genesis 26:34-35*
2. Rebekah's plot to deceive Isaac. *Genesis 27:1-17*
3. Isaac blesses Jacob instead of Esau. *Genesis 27:18-40*
4. Jacob flees from Esau toward Haran. *Genesis 27:41—28:9*
5. Jacob's dream in Bethel. *Genesis 28:10-22*
6. Jacob in Haran, with his uncle Laban. *Genesis 29:1-14*
7. The faith of Isaac. *Hebrews 11:20*

A proverb: Better is a dry morsel with quiet than a house full of feasting with strife. *Proverbs 17:1*

A prayer: Lord, forgive us for the times we have deceived others. Thank you for even making good come from such situations.

Day 14

Jacob forms a family with abundance in Haran

1. Jacob marries Leah, then Rachel. *Genesis 29:15-30*
2. Jacob's children. *Genesis 29:31—30:24*
3. The increase of Jacob's flock. *Genesis 30:25-43*
4. Jacob plans to leave Haran. *Genesis 31:1-16*
5. The love and faithfulness of God. *Psalm 138:1-8*

A proverb: The blessing of the Lord makes rich, and he adds no sorrow with it. *Proverbs 10:22*

A prayer: We praise you, O God, for you have exalted us through Jesus Christ, and you have walked with us in the midst of trouble. May your purpose be fulfilled in us.

Day 15

Jacob returns to Canaan and encounters Esau

1. Jacob flees, with Laban in pursuit. *Genesis 31:17-55*
2. Jacob prepares to meet Esau. *Genesis 32:1-21*
3. Jacob wrestles with God. *Genesis 32:22-32*
4. The encounter of Jacob and Esau. *Genesis 33:1-17*

A proverb: The human mind plans the way, but the Lord directs the steps. *Proverbs 16:9*

A prayer: Lord, help us handle situations in our lives that we fear. Give us courage to go forward into the unknown with the knowledge that you are with us.

Day 16

Jacob and family in Shechem, then in Bethel

1. Jacob in Shechem. *Genesis 33:18-20*
2. Dinah raped; her marriage plans. *Genesis 34:1-24*
3. Slaughter of the Shechemites. *Genesis 34:25-31*
4. Bethel: God renews covenant with Jacob. *Genesis 35:1-15*
5. The death of Rachel and Isaac. *Genesis 35:16-29*
6. Descendants of Esau. *Genesis 36:1-19; 1 Chronicles 1:35-37*

A proverb: Do not say, "I will repay evil"; wait for the Lord, and he will help you. *Proverbs 20:22*

A prayer: O Lord, help us to see the futility of vengeance. Forgive us when we have wronged others or try to get even. Teach us your way of love and peace.

Day 17

Difficulties within Israel's family

1. The sons of Israel. *1 Chronicles 2:1-2*
2. Joseph's dreams. *Genesis 37:1-11*
3. Joseph is sold by his brothers. *Genesis 37:12-36*
4. The wickedness of the sons of Judah. *Genesis 38:1-11*
5. Judah and his daughter-in-law Tamar. *Genesis 38:12-30*
6. Joseph in the house of Potiphar. *Genesis 39:1-23*

A proverb: Like a gold ring in a pig's snout is a beautiful woman without good sense. *Proverbs 11:22*

A prayer: Forgive us, Lord, for favoritism, bragging, deceitfulness, and improper behavior with the opposite sex. Thank you for pardon, for restoration, and for using imperfect people.

Day 18

Joseph becomes ruler of Egypt

1. Dreams of cupbearer and baker. *Genesis 40:1-23*
2. Joseph interprets Pharaoh's dreams. *Genesis 41:1-36*
3. Joseph is made ruler of all Egypt. *Genesis 41:37-57*

A proverb: On the lips of one who has understanding wisdom is found, but a rod is for the back of one who lacks sense. *Proverbs 10:13*

A prayer: Lord, may your Spirit help us discern your ways. Give us the gift of prophecy that we may share your truths with our fellow Christians in a fitting and orderly way.

Day 19

Brothers of Joseph visit Egypt to buy food

1. Ten brothers arrive. *Genesis 42:1-17*
2. Simeon held in custody. *Genesis 42:18-26*
3. Nine brothers return to Jacob. *Genesis 42:27-38*
4. Jacob finally permits second trip. *Genesis 43:1-14*
5. Joseph receives the nine plus Benjamin. *Genesis 43:15-34*
6. The brothers sent on their way. *Genesis 44:1-3*

A proverb: Whoever walks in integrity walks securely, but whoever follows perverse ways will be found out. *Proverbs 10:9*

A prayer: Lord, teach us how to deal with evildoers. Convict them of their wrong, and let them turn to follow righteousness and mercy.

Day 20

Joseph reveals himself to his brothers

1. Joseph's cup found in Benjamin's sack. *Genesis 44:4-13*
2. They return to Joseph; Judah's plea. *Gen. 44:14-34*
3. Joseph finally reveals himself. *Genesis 45:1-15*
4. Pharaoh sends them back with supplies. *Genesis 45:16-28*
5. Israel goes to Egypt with all his family. *Genesis 46:1-27*

A proverb: The Lord has made everything for its purpose, even the wicked for the day of trouble. *Proverbs 16:4*

A prayer: Thank you, Lord, for working out so many things in our lives and for the way you have used others to be a blessing to us.

Day 21

Jacob and his family in Egypt

1. Jacob's family established in Goshen. *Genesis 46:28—47:12*
2. Joseph's policy during the famine. *Genesis 47:13-26*
3. Jacob's sojourn in Egypt. *Genesis 47:27-31*
4. Jacob blesses Manasseh and Ephraim. *Genesis 48:1-22*
5. God's dealing with his people. *Psalm 105:1-25*

A proverb: Grandchildren are the crown of the aged, and the glory of children is their parents. *Proverbs 17:6*

A prayer: We thank you, God, for the blessings we have received from our parents. Help us be a blessing to our own children and to all of those in the family of God.

Day 22

The final years of Jacob and Joseph

1. Jacob blesses his sons. *Genesis 49:1-28*
2. Jacob dies, is buried in Canaan. *Gen. 49:29—50:14*
3. Joseph reassures his brothers. *Genesis 50:15-21*
4. The death of Joseph. *Genesis 50:22-26*
5. The faith of Jacob and Joseph. *Hebrews 11:21-22*
6. The growth of Israel in Egypt. *Exodus 1:1-7*
7. How God protects his people *Psalm 91:1-16*

A proverb: Gray hair is a crown of glory; it is gained in a righteous life. *Proverbs 16:31*

A prayer: Thank you, God, for those faithful to you in their old age. Help us to honor them, learn from them, and respect their wishes. If in your mercy you give us a long life, may we be faithful till the end.

Day 23

The afflictions and calamities of Job
1. Job and his family. *Job 1:1-5*
2. Satan's first test for Job. *Job 1:6-22*
3. Satan's second test for Job. *Job 2:2-10*
4. Job's friends. *Job 2:11-13*
5. Job deplores his condition. *Job 3:1-26*
6. The cry of an afflicted person. *Psalm 88:1-18*

A proverb: The human spirit will endure sickness; but a broken spirit—who can bear? *Proverbs 18:14*

A prayer: O Lord, we confess that we are often depressed. Help us to understand how the evil one can discourage us. Give us faith to believe that you know and see us in our suffering.

Day 24

Eliphaz, Job's friend, reprimands him, and Job responds
1. Eliphaz tries to explain suffering and urges Job to call out to God and to accept God's correction. *Job 4:1—5:27*
2. Job expresses his anguish and, in distress, puts many questions to God and to his friends. *Job 6:1—7:21*

A proverb: Desire without knowledge is not good, and one who moves too hurriedly misses the way. *Proverbs 19:2*

A prayer: We call to you, O Lord, in time of pain and suffering. Help us be true friends to others who are suffering. May we be willing to accept pain in the midst of our anguish.

Day 25

Friend Bildad gives counsel; Job responds

1. Bildad tries to explain the justice of God: sin brings punishment, and uprightness brings prosperity. *Job 8:1-22*
2. Job replies to Eliphaz, recognizes God's wisdom, does not pretend to argue with God, proclaims his innocence in the midst of his suffering, and asks for an advocate before God. *Job 9:1—10:22*
3. A prayer of one in anguish. *Psalm 39:1-13*

A proverb: The crucible is for silver, and the furnace is for gold, so a person is tested by being praised. *Proverbs 27:21*

A prayer: O Creator God, we recognize how brief our life is compared to your infinity. Show us the way to live that brings honor and glory to you.

Day 26

Zophar, Job's third friend, also reprimands him

1. Zophar directly accuses Job of wrong but claims that God will restore him if he puts away sin. *Job 11:1-20*
2. Job claims the same ability to understand God. He speaks of the wisdom of God but still demands an answer from God even though he recognizes his own limitations. *Job 12:1—13:28*
3. Hope in God! *Psalm 42:1-11*

A proverb: One is commended for good sense, but a perverse mind is despised. *Proverbs 12:8*

A prayer: Our hearts thirst for you, O God. Our lives are in your hands. We come in confidence before you to ask for your presence and your blessing.

Day 27

Job's friends continue their accusations

1. Eliphaz rebukes Job for questioning God, and says Job's sin brings his suffering. *Job 15:1-35*
2. Job accuses his friends of being miserable comforters and maintains his innocence even though he is losing hope. *Job 16:1—17:16*
3. Bildad takes offense and reaffirms that Job's sin brings his suffering. *Job 18:1-21*

A proverb: A scoffer seeks wisdom in vain, but knowledge is easy for one who understands. *Proverbs 14:6*

A prayer: O Lord, forgive us for sometimes bringing others misery rather than comfort. Forgive us for accusing others of sin when they suffer.

Day 28

Job continues his response to his friends

1. Job rejects his friends' rebukes and accuses them of helping destroy and alienate him. He pleads for pity and expresses faith in God. *Job 19:1-29*
2. Zophar is offended and reaffirms that the wicked always fall into punishment. *Job 20:1-29*
3. Job observs how many wicked people prosper. Who can tell God what to do? What his friends say is not true. *Job 21:1-34*

A proverb: It is the wisdom of the clever to understand where they go, but the folly of fools misleads. *Proverbs 14:8*

A prayer: We honor you, O God, for your wisdom and sovereignty. Work in our lives with mercy and love.

Day 29

Last arguments of Eliphaz and Bildad

1. Eliphaz: Job's wickedness is great. He cannot hide from God and should repent. *Job 22:1-30*
2. Job reasserts his righteousness but desires a personal hearing and asks for a time of judgment. Sinners will face death. *Job 23:1—24:25*
3. Bildad: Righteousness is impossible. *Job 25:1-6*
4. The judgment of God. *Psalm 82:1-8*

A proverb: One who justifies the wicked and one who condemns the righteous are both alike an abomination to the Lord. *Proverbs 17:15*

A prayer: We thank you, God, that we can trust your judgment. Thank you for salvation from sin and death through your Son, Jesus Christ.

Day 30

Job responds and proclaims God's wisdom

1. Job rejects his friends' arguments and says he will always maintain his integrity. He speaks of the fate of the wicked. *Job 26:1—27:23*
2. A poem about the wisdom of God. *Job 28:1-28*
3. A beatitude about wisdom. *Proverbs 3:13-18*
4. The judgment of One with wisdom and understanding. *Isaiah 11:1-9*
5. A psalm of praise. *Psalm 92:1-15*

A proverb: The wise of heart is called perceptive, and pleasant speech increases persuasiveness. *Proverbs 16:21*

A prayer: We praise you, Lord, for your understanding and faithfulness. Help us know your wisdom.

Day 31

Job reviews his life

1. Job remembers his previous prosperity. *Job 29:1-25*
2. Job tells of his lost dignity and his lost health. *Job 30:1-31*
3. Job proclaims his moral integrity. *Job 31:1-40*

A proverb: The glory of youths is their strength, but the beauty of the aged is their gray hair. *Proverbs 20:29*

A prayer: O Lord, help us live with integrity, as Job did. Forgive us when we have mistreated the poor and the needy. Teach us to be faithful to you, to our family, and to everyone around us.

Day 32

The beginning of Elihu's discourse

1. Elihu, a younger man, speaks after the older friends of Job have finished. *Job 32:1-22*
2. Elihu expresses his concern for Job and tells him that he is wrong to say he is without sin. *Job 33:1-30*
3. Elihu asks Job and his friends to listen. God cannot do evil, nor does God accept an insincere confession. *Job 33:31—34:33*

A proverb: The mind of one who has understanding seeks knowledge, but the mouths of fools feed on folly. *Proverbs 15:14*

A prayer: O Lord, forgive us for insincere confessions. Help us to be honest with you, with ourselves, and with others. We want to leave our selfish ways and seek your will.

Day 33

Elihu continues his discourse

1. Elihu accuses Job of rebellion, says talking to God is useless. _Job 34:34—35:16_
2. Elihu teaches that God rules justly. _Job 36:1-15_
3. Elihu says wickedness brings affliction. He exalts God's power. _Job 36:16-26_
4. Elihu sees God's power in lightning and rain-storms. _Job 36:27—37:24_
5. The glory of God in a storm. _Psalm 29:1-11_

A proverb: With their mouths the godless would destroy their neighbors, but by knowledge the righteous are delivered. _Proverbs 11:9_

A prayer: We praise you, Lord, for your power and glory seen in nature. Thank you for sharing your power and glory through your Spirit in our lives.

Day 34

God's response to Job

1. God asks Job questions about Creation showing the wisdom and power of God. Questions give way to one unspoken answer. _Job 38:1—39:30_
2. Job responds. _Job 40:1-5_
3. God asks Job more questions concerning divine justice. _Job 40:6-24_

A proverb: A person's pride will bring humiliation, but one who is lowly in spirit will obtain honor. _Proverbs 29:23_

A prayer: We recognize our unworthiness before you, almighty God. Forgive us for questioning your work in the world. Thank you for giving worth to our lives through Jesus Christ.

Day 35

Job's restoration

1. God continues questioning Job, using the Leviathan as an illustration of his power. *Job 41:1-34*
2. Job finally repents, not of his sins but of his questions and demands to God. *Job 42:1-6*
3. The later life of Job. *Job 42:7-17*
4. Two psalms of gratitude. *Psalm 34:1-22; Psalm 40:1-17*

A proverb: The rich and the poor have this in common; the Lord is the maker of them all. *Proverbs 22:2*

A prayer: We too extol and praise you, Lord, for your goodness. We thank you for your salvation and for your protection. Help us be faithful stewards of your blessings.

Day 36

The birth and call of Moses

1. The oppression of the Israelites. *Exodus 1:8-22*
2. The birth of Moses. *Exodus 2:1-10*
3. Moses' escape from Egypt. *Exodus 2:11-22*
4. The slavery of the Israelites; the call of Moses. *Exodus 2:23—4:17*
5. The faith of Moses. *Hebrews 11:23-27*

A proverb: One who is clever conceals knowledge, but the mind of a fool broadcasts folly. *Proverbs 12:23*

A prayer: Thank you, Lord, because we know that you see us when we are in distress and are interested in our well-being. Give us patience to wait on you. Thank you for those you have called to bring deliverance and justice.

Day 37

The Lord to Pharoah: Let my people go!

1. Moses returns to Egypt. *Exodus 4:18-31*
2. First encounter with Pharaoh. *Exodus 5:1-5*
3. Pharaoh reacts. Israel complains. *Exodus 5:6-21*
4. God promises deliverance. *Exodus 5:22—6:13*
5. The families of the Israelites. *Exodus 6:14-25*
6. Aaron speaks for Moses. *Exodus 6:26—7:7*
7. Second encounter with Pharaoh. *Exodus 7:8-13*

A proverb: Better to meet a she-bear robbed of its cubs than to confront a fool immersed in folly. *Proverbs 17:12*

A prayer: Lord, we thank you for your promises. Give us faith to believe in your Word.

Day 38

The first seven plagues upon Egypt

1. Water to blood. Magicians copied. *Exodus 7:14-24*
2. Frogs. Pharaoh hardened his heart. *Exodus 8:1-15*
3. Gnats. Magicians could not copy. *Exodus 8:16-19*
4. Flies. Pharaoh hardened his heart. *Exodus 8:20-32*
5. Egyptians' animals diseased. *Exodus 9:1-7*
6. Boils. The Lord hardened Pharaoh's heart. *Exodus 9:8-12*
7. Hail. Pharaoh reneged. *Exodus 9:13-35*

A proverb: One who is often reproved, yet remains stubborn, will suddenly be broken beyond healing. *Proverbs 29:1*

A prayer: Forgive us, Lord, for the times we are stubborn-hearted. Help us to accept your discipline in our lives and to seek and know your will.

Day 39

Final plagues. Passover instituted

1. The plague of Locusts. *Exodus 10:1-20*
2. The plague of darkness. *Exodus 10:21-29*
3. Death of firstborn announced. *Exodus 11:1-10*
4. Institution of the Passover: *Exodus 12:1-28*
5. Egyptian firstborn die; Israel's exit. *Exodus 12:29-36*
6. The work of God. *Psalm 105:26-36*

A proverb: All those who are arrogant are an abomination to the Lord; be assured, they will not go unpunished. *Proverbs 16:5*

A prayer: We thank you, Lord, for your salvation, for your liberation from all kinds of oppression. May we be faithful to you and follow your leading.

Day 40

The exodus. Instructions for Passover

1. Rameses to Succoth. *Exodus 12:37-42*
2. Instructions for the Passover. *Exodus 12:43—13:16*
3. Later Passover instructions. *Leviticus 23:4-8; Numbers 28:16-25; Deuteronomy 16:1-8*
4. Passover in Sinai. *Numbers 9:1-14*
5. Jesus celebrates the Passover. *Matthew 26:17-29*
6. The faith of Moses. *Hebrews 11:28*

A proverb: Those who are attentive to a matter will prosper, and happy are those who trust in the Lord. *Proverbs 16:20*

A prayer: We praise you, God, for saving us through the blood of Jesus Christ that was shed for us. Give us faith to go forward, trusting your promises.

Day 41

The crossing of the Red Sea

1. Pillars of cloud and fire. *Exodus 13:17-22*
2. Crossing the Red Sea. *Exodus 14:1-31*
3. The song of Moses and Miriam. *Exodus 15:1-21*
4. Saved by faith. *Hebrews 11:29*
5. Praise for God's salvation. *Psalm 136:1-15*
6. Let everything praise the Lord. *Psalm 150:1-6*

A proverb: Trust in the Lord with all your heart, and do not rely on your own insight. *Proverbs 3:5*

A prayer: We thank you, Lord, for giving us victory over sin and evil. May your presence guide us always. Give us faith to follow and to obey.

Day 42

The march in the desert

1. From the Red Sea to Marah and to Elim. *Exodus 15:22-27*
2. God provides manna and quail. *Exodus 16:1-36*
3. God provides water from the rock of Horeb. *Exodus 17:1-7*
4. Defeat of the Amalekites. *Exodus 17:8-16*
5. Summary of the journey thus far. *Numbers 33:1-15*
6. The providence of God. *Psalm 105:37-45*

A proverb: The greedy person stirs up strife, but whoever trusts in the Lord will be enriched. *Proverbs 28:25*

A prayer: Thank you, God, for giving us water and food in abundance. Help us be faithful stewards of these good gifts and learn how to share with those who do not have enough food and water.

Day 43

Help for Moses. The letter to Titus

1. Jethro's visit to Moses and his advice. *Exodus 18:1-27*
2. God provides help for Moses. *Deuteronomy 1:9-18*
3. Paul instructs Titus to name elders. *Titus 1:1-16*
4. Paul instructs Titus to teach. *Titus 2:1-15*
5. Paul's final instructions to Titus. *Titus 3:1-15*

A proverb: Without counsel, plans go wrong, but with many advisers they succeed. *Proverbs 15:22*

A prayer: O Lord, we are thankful for those who have counseled us. Guide us in finding others to assist in the things you have given us to do. May we also be willing to help our leaders.

Day 44

God covenants with Israel and gives the law

1. God announces his covenant at Mount Sinai. *Exodus 19:1-25*
2. The fear of the people. *Exodus 20:18-21*
3. Confirmation of the covenant. *Exodus 24:1-18; 31:18*
4. Moses remembers how it happened. *Deuteronomy 5:1-5, 22-33*
5. A warning for Christians. *Hebrews 12:18-29*

A proverb: An intelligent mind acquires knowledge, and the ear of the wise seeks knowledge. *Proverbs 18:15*

A prayer: We want to listen to your voice, O God. Forgive us when we have ignored your commands. We come before you with awe because of your holiness and power. Help us live holy lives before you.

Day 45

Impatience and apostasy of the Israelites

1. The golden calf. *Exodus 32:1-35*
2. Moses remembers what happened. *Deuteronomy 9:7-21, 25-29*
3. Isaiah later warns Israel of their idolatry. *Isaiah 56:9—57:13*

A proverb: Doing wrong is like sport to a fool, but wise conduct is pleasure to a person of understanding. *Proverbs 10:23*

A prayer: Forgive us, Lord, when we have participated in pagan revelry that is not pleasing to you. We want to find our joy in celebration that honors you. Thank you for giving us strength in time of temptation.

Day 46

The covenant renewed

1. God promises his presence. *Exodus 33:1-23*
2. God promises the help of his angel. *Exodus 23:20-33*
3. The new tablets of the law. *Exodus 34:1-16, 27-35*
4. Moses remembers how it happened. *Deuteronomy 10:1-5, 10-11*
5. Forgiveness and restoration of God. *Psalm 85:1-13*

A proverb: Cease straying, my child, from the words of knowledge, in order that you may hear instruction. *Proverbs 19:27*

A prayer: How wonderful are your promises, O God. May your presence ever lead and guide us. May your angel go before us, and may your Word be eternal light on our path.

Day 47

The first of the Ten Commandments

1. The Lord alone is God. *Exod. 20:1-3; Deut. 5:6-7*
2. Worship only the Lord. *Exodus 22:20; 23:13*
3. The Lord our God is one. *Deuteronomy 6:1-25*
4. Keep God's commandments. *Deuteronomy 11:1-32*
5. There is no other god. *Isaiah 44:6-8*
6. The first and great commandment. *Matthew 22:34-40*
7. How I love your law. *Psalm 119:97-104*

A proverb: Those who keep the commandment will live; those who are heedless of their ways will die. *Proverbs 19:16*

A prayer: O Lord, your truth is wonderful! We honor only you, not other gods or powers of this world.

Day 48

The second commandment

1. Do not worship idols. *Exod. 20:4-6; Deut. 5:8-10*
2. Idols and altars; idols prohibited. *Exodus 20:22-26; 34:17; Leviticus 19:4; 26:1*
3. Warnings against worshiping other gods. *Deuteronomy 4:15-19; 12:29—13:18*
4. Death for the idol worshiper. *Deut. 16:21—17:7*
5. The folly of idol worship. *Isaiah 44:9-20*
6. About food sacrificed to idols. *1 Corinthians 8:1-13*
7. Trust in God, not in idols. *Psalm 115:1-11*

A proverb: Those who walk uprightly fear the Lord, but one who is devious in conduct despises him. *Proverbs 14:2*

A prayer: Forgive us, ever-living God, for trusting in dead things. Our loyalty is only to you.

Day 49

Third and fourth commandments

1. No swearing! *Exodus 20:7; Deuteronomy 5:11*
2. Punishment for blasphemy. *Leviticus 24:10-16, 23*
3. Do not swear! *Matthew 5:33-37; 23:16-22; James 5:12*
4. Keep the Sabbath! *Exodus 20:8-11; Deuteronomy 5:12-15*
5. Sabbath laws. *Exodus 23:10-12; 31:12-17; 34:21; 35:1-3; Leviticus 23:1-3; 26:2*
6. Promises for observing the Sabbath. *Isaiah 56:1-8; 58:13-14*
7. Jesus on the Sabbath. *Matt. 12:1-13; Luke 13:10-17*

A proverb: When one will not listen to the law, even one's prayers are an abomination. *Proverbs 28:9*

A prayer: O God, forgive us for making wrongful use of your name or neglecting a rhythm of rest. May we discern your will for these matters.

Day 50

Fifth and seventh commandments

1. Honor parents! *Exodus 20:12; Deuteronomy 5:16*
2. Respect for parents. *Leviticus 19:1-3; 20:9*
3. Three proverbs. *Proverbs 15:20; 19:26; 20:20*
4. Sincere honor of father and mother. *Matthew 15:1-9*
5. No adultery! *Exodus 20:14; Deuteronomy 5:18*
6. Unlawful sexual relations. *Lev. 18:1-30; 20:10-24*
7. Moses and Jesus on divorce. *Deut. 24:1-4; Matthew 5:27-32; 19:1-12*

A proverb: Train children in the right way, and when old, they will not stray. *Proverbs 22:6*

A prayer: Give us strong families, O Lord, where there is respect, honor, and faithfulness.

Day 51

Sixth and ninth commandments

1. Do not murder! *Exodus 20:13; Deuteronomy 5:17*
2. On personal injury and retaliation. *Exodus 21:12-36; Leviticus 24:17-22*
3. Jesus' teaching on violence. *Matthew 5:21-26, 38-48*
4. No false witness! *Exodus 20:16; Deuteronomy 5:20*
5. Falsehood prohibited. *Exodus 23:1-9; Deuteronomy 22:1-4*
6. Against slandering and boasting. *James 4:11-17*
7. God is strong and loving. *Psalm 62:1-12*

A proverb: When the ways of people please the Lord, he causes even their enemies to be at peace with them. *Proverbs 16:7*

A prayer: Lord, forgive us for our violence and dishonesty. Teach us your ways of peace and integrity.

Day 52

Eighth and tenth commandments

1. No stealing! *Exodus 20:15; Deuteronomy 5:19*
2. Laws of restitution. *Exodus 22:1-15*
3. Three proverbs. *Proverbs 16:11; 20:10, 23*
4. No coveting! *Exodus 20:17; Deuteronomy 5:21*
5. Humanitarian laws. *Exodus 22:21-31; Lev. 19:9-18*
6. The good Samaritan. *Luke 10:25-37*
7. Anxiety and riches. *Matthew 6:19-34.*
8. Evil comes from the heart. *Mark 7:20-23*

A proverb: Do not boast about tomorrow, for you do not know what a day may bring. *Proverbs 27:1*

A prayer: O Lord, we confess our covetous desires. Help us to be satisfied with what we have, avoid boasting, and strive first for your righteousness.

Day 53

Offerings and artisans for the tabernacle

1. Instructions for the offering. *Exodus 25:1-9*
2. Generous offerings for the tabernacle. *Exodus 35:4-29*
3. The naming of artisans. *Exodus 31:1-11*
4. The artisans receive the offerings. *Exodus 35:30—36:7*
5. Materials used. *Exodus 38:21-31*
6. Thanksgiving to God. *Psalm 118:1-14*

A proverb: All day long the wicked covet, but the righteous give and do not hold back. *Proverbs 21:26*

A prayer: We thank you, Lord, for the way you have blessed us. We want to be faithful stewards of your gifts and give for the building of your kingdom and your church.

Day 54

The furniture for the tabernacle

1. The ark. *Exodus 25:10-22; 37:1-9*
2. The table. *Exodus 25:23-30; 37:10-16*
3. The lampstand. *Exodus 25:31-40; 37:17-24*
4. The altar of incense. *Exodus 30:1-10; 37:25-28*
5. Oil for the lamps. *Exodus 27:20-21; Leviticus 24:1-4*
6. Instructions for lighting the lamps. *Numbers 8:1-4*
7. A psalm of David. *Psalm 15:1-5*

A proverb: In the house of the righteous there is much treasure, but trouble befalls the income of the wicked. *Proverbs 15:6*

A prayer: Teach us holy living, O Lord, that we may be a blessing for others and an honor to your name. May our worship attract others to you.

Day 55

Construction of the tabernacle.
Hebrews, chapter 2

1. Instructions to build the tabernacle. *Exod. 26:1-37*
2. Building according to God's instructions. *Exodus 36:8-38*
3. Jesus, a true man. (Following readings include Hebrews, chapters 2—10.) *Hebrews 2:5-18*

A proverb: The appetite of workers works for them; their hunger urges them on. *Proverbs 16:26*

A prayer: We thank you, O God, that in your wisdom you gave us your Son, Jesus Christ, who was like us in every way, to be our Savior and Lord. May we be faithful to your commands in our work and in our service.

Day 56

The courtyard and the altar. Hebrews, chapter 3

1. The courtyard. *Exodus 27:9-19; 38:9-20*
2. The altar of burnt offering. *Exodus 27:1-8; 38:1-7*
3. The basin for washing. *Exodus 30:17-21; 38:8*
4. The anointing oil. *Exodus 30:22-33*
5. The incense. *Exodus 30:34-38; 37:29*
6. The sacred bread. *Leviticus 24:5-9*
7. Jesus is greater than Moses. *Hebrews 3:1-19*

A proverb: The sated appetite spurns honey, but to a ravenous appetite even the bitter is sweet. *Proverbs 27:7*

A prayer: O Lord, we are thankful for the faithfulness of Moses and the faithfulness of Jesus. Speak to us today, that we might know your salvation. Forgive us when we turn away.

Day 57

The priestly garments. Hebrews, chapter 4
1. Instructions for priestly garments. *Exodus 28:1-43*
2. Making the priestly garments. *Exodus 39:1-31*
3. A Sabbath rest for God's people. *Hebrews 4:1-13*

A proverb: Listen to advice and accept instruction, that you may gain wisdom for the future. *Proverbs 19:20*

A prayer: We thank you, Lord, for your Word, which has penetrated our lives and laid bare all of our thoughts and actions. We confess our shortcomings. We express our faith in Jesus Christ and hold firmly to your promise that we will enter the rest prepared for us.

Day 58

**The finishing of the tabernacle.
Hebrews, chapter 5**
1. Moses inspects the work. *Exodus 39:32-43*
2. The tabernacle is set up. *Exodus 40:1-33*
3. The atonement offering. *Exodus 30:11-16*
4. The glory of the Lord in the tabernacle. *Exodus 40:34-38; Numbers 9:15-23*
5. Christ is superior to Aaron. *Hebrews 4:14—5:14*

A proverb: In all toil there is profit, but mere talk leads only to poverty. *Proverbs 14:23*

A prayer: O Lord, we approach your throne of grace with confidence in the name of Jesus Christ, our High Priest, who also paid our atonement offering. For this we honor you and express our desire to share this good news with others.

Day 59

Dedication of the tabernacle and the offerings of each tribe

1. The dedication of the tabernacle. _Numbers 7:1-11_
2. The offerings given by each tribe. For 12 days, leaders of each tribe brought the same offering but on different days. _Numbers 7:12-83_
3. Summary of the offerings. _Numbers 7:84-89_

A proverb: Whoever gives to the poor will lack nothing, but one who turns a blind eye will get many a curse. _Proverbs 28:27_

A prayer: We thank you, Lord, for the presence of your Spirit in the midst of your people. With our offerings, we want to share in your work in our midst. Bless those who administer and use these offerings for your glory.

Day 60

The burnt and grain offerings. Hebrews, chapter 6

1. The burnt offering. _Leviticus 1:1-17_
2. Rules for the burnt offering. _Leviticus 6:8-13_
3. The grain offering. _Leviticus 2:1-16_
4. Rules for the grain offering. _Leviticus 6:14-23_
5. The daily offerings. _Exodus 29:38-46; Numbers 28:1-8_
6. A warning to Christians. _Hebrews 6:1-20_

A proverb: Be assured, the wicked will not go unpunished, but those who are righteous will escape. _Proverbs 11:21_

A prayer: We confess our sins, O Lord, believing that Jesus died and shed his blood for us on the cross. Keep us from falling away and losing faith.

Day 61

The fellowship offering. Hebrews, chapter 7

1. The fellowship offering. *Leviticus 3:1-17*
2. Regulations for the fellowship offering. *Leviticus 7:11-21; 19:5-8*
3. Regulations for the priests. *Lev. 7:28-36; 10:8-20*
4. Sabbath and monthly offerings. *Numbers 28:9-15*
5. The eternal priesthood of Christ. *Hebrews 7:11-28*

A proverb: Better is a dinner of vegetables where love is than a fatted ox and hatred with it. *Proverbs 15:17*

A prayer: We thank you, Lord, for your Son, who is our High Priest forever. We also thank you for the fellowship of the people of God. Help us to share with one another as well as with those who minister to us.

Day 62

The sin and guilt offerings

1. The sin offering. *Leviticus 4:1-35*
2. Regulations for the sin offering. *Leviticus 6:24-30*
3. The guilt offering. *Leviticus 5:14-6:7*
4. Regulations for the guilt offering. *Lev. 7:1-10; 37-38*
5. Several reasons for guilt. *Leviticus 5:1-6*
6. Sin and guilt offerings of the poor. *Leviticus 5:7-13*

A proverb: The desire of the righteous ends only in good; the expectation of the wicked in wrath. *Proverbs 11:23*

A prayer: We thank you, O God, that in Christ we have an offering for sin. Thank you for your forgiveness and mercy. May we learn to flee from sin and follow your righteousness.

Day 63

The consecration of the priests.
Hebrews, chapter 8

1. Instructions for the consecration of the priests.
   Exodus 29:1-37
2. The consecration of Aaron. *Leviticus 8:1-30*
3. The High Priest of a new covenant. *Hebrews 8:1-13*

A proverb: Commit your work to the Lord, and
your plans will be established. *Proverbs 16:3*

A prayer: We thank you, Lord, for a High Priest of a
new and better covenant, who is seated at your
right hand in heaven. We come to you in confidence that you know our needs and our longings.

Day 64

The first sacrifices. Hebrews, chapter 9

1. Aaron and his sons complete their consecration.
   Leviticus 8:31-36
2. The first sacrifices for the people. *Leviticus 9:1-24*
3. The disobedience of Nadab and Abihu. *Leviticus
   10:1-7*
4. Sacrifices outside the tabernacle prohibited.
   Leviticus 17:1-9
5. Unacceptable sacrifices. *Leviticus 22:17-30*
6. Christ is our sacrifice. *Hebrews 9:1-28*

A proverb: The way of the wicked is an abomination to the Lord, but he loves the one who pursues
righteousness. *Proverbs 15:9*

A prayer: We thank you, Lord, for the forgiveness of
our sins by the blood of Christ, who has entered the
heavenly tabernacle once and for all. Guide us in
newness of life so that we may have victory over sin.

Day 65

The Day of Atonement. Hebrews, chapter 10

1. The sacrifice on the Day of Atonement. *Leviticus 16:1-34*
2. The Day of Atonement is a special feast. *Leviticus 23:26-32*
3. Offerings on the Day of Atonement. *Numbers 29:7-11*
4. A superior and eternal covenant. *Hebrews 10:1-39*

A proverb: Fools mock at the guilt offering, but the upright enjoy God's favor. *Proverbs 14:9*

A prayer: We enter your presence with confidence and faith. Thank you, Lord, for salvation and for the privilege of coming to you freely in prayer. Guide us as we meet together with other Christians that we may encourage one another.

Day 66

Laws of holiness—clean and unclean food

1. Unclean animals prohibited as food. *Leviticus 11:1-47; 20:25-26*
2. Moses repeats these prohibitions. *Deuteronomy 14:1-21*
3. Eating fat and blood prohibited. *Leviticus 7:22-27; 17:10-16*
4. Other prohibitions. *Exodus 34:25-26*

A proverb: Those who keep the law are wise children, but companions of gluttons shame their parents. *Proverbs 28:7*

A prayer: Thank you, generous God, for the food you give us daily. Forgive us for the sin of gluttony, and help us discern what nourishment is healthy.

Day 67

Laws of holiness—infectious skin diseases
1. Instructions for diagnosis of skin diseases. *Leviticus 13:1-46*
2. Cleansing from infectious skin diseases. *Leviticus 14:1-32*
3. Skin diseases excluded from the camp. *Num. 5:1-4*
4. Moses reminds the people of these instructions. *Deuteronomy 24:8-9*

A proverb: By mere words servants are not disciplined, for though they understand, they will not give heed. *Proverbs 29:19*

A prayer: O Lord, we thank you for healthy bodies. We also thank you for those who heal our bodies. Help us to take care of our bodies in such a way that our lives can be a glory and honor to your name.

Day 68

Laws of holiness. Norms for purification
1. Purification after childbirth. *Leviticus 12:1-8*
2. Purification after discharges. *Leviticus 15:1-18*
3. Purification after menstruation. *Leviticus 15:19-33*
4. Regulations about mildew. *Leviticus 13:47-59*
5. Cleansing from mildew. *Leviticus 14:33-57*
6. Norms during wartime. *Deuteronomy 23:9-14*

A proverb: The wise woman builds her house, but the foolish tears it down with her own hands. *Proverbs 14:1*

A prayer: We praise you, God, for your holiness. Cleanse our lives and make us holy as you are holy. Show us those things which we should remove from our lives.

Day 69

Instructions for priests. 1 Corinthians, chapter 7
1. Rules of cleanliness for priests. *Leviticus 21:1-24*
2. Rules of ceremonial cleanliness for priests.
   Leviticus 22:1-16
3. Sacrifices to Molech prohibited. *Leviticus 20:1-5*
4. Paul's advice regarding marriage. *1 Cor. 7:1-40*

A proverb: House and wealth are inherited from parents, but a prudent wife is from the Lord. *Proverbs 19:14*

A prayer: Thank you, God, for Christian families. Forgive us for all the uncleanness that enters our lives. May your Spirit guide us in the decisions we make daily in our families.

Day 70

The three principal annual festivals
1. General instructions for the three festivals. *Exodus 23:14-19; 34:18, 22-24* (Instructions for the feast of unleavened bread were read on day 40.)
2. The Feast of Weeks, Pentecost. *Leviticus 23:9-22; Numbers 28:26-31; Deuteronomy 16:9-12*
3. The Feast of Tabernacles. *Leviticus 23:33-44; Numbers 29:12-40; Deuteronomy 16:13-17*

A proverb: The righteous have enough to satisfy their appetite, but the belly of the wicked is empty. *Proverbs 13:25*

A prayer: Lord, help us learn how to celebrate your great acts in history. May our observance of Christmas, Easter, and Thanksgiving be sincere expressions of our love and gratefulness for your mercy and your many gifts to us.

Day 71

The sabbatical year and the year of Jubilee
1. The Sabbath year. *Leviticus 25:1-7*
2. The year of Jubilee. *Leviticus 25:8-24*
3. Property redemption. *Leviticus 25:25-38*
4. Mediums and spiritists prohibited. *Leviticus 20:6-8, 27; Deuteronomy 18:9-14*
5. Various laws. *Exodus 22:16-19; Leviticus 19:19-37; Deuteronomy 22:5-12*
6. Laws of restitution. *Numbers 5:5-10*
7. The blessing of keeping the Law. *Psalm 119:1-8*

A proverb: A slave who deals wisely will rule over a child who acts shamefully, and will share the inheritance as one of the family. *Proverbs 17:2*

A prayer: O Lord, we praise you for the wisdom of your Law. Help us learn humanitarian concern. Forgive us for selfishness and individualism. Teach us to forgive others and to share.

Day 72

Instructions regarding vows and redemption
1. The vow of the Nazirite. *Numbers 6:1-21*
2. Vows within the family. *Numbers 30:1-16*
3. Redeeming what is vowed to the Lord. *Leviticus 27:1-34*
4. Teach me your statutes. *Psalm 119:33-48*

A proverb: If one gives answer before hearing, it is folly and shame. *Proverbs 18:13*

A prayer: We want to keep our promises, O Lord. Forgive us when we have not been faithful to you or to those with whom we live.

Day 73

Promises and warning. Hebrews, chapter 13

1. Keep the commands. *Leviticus 22:31-33*
2. Reward for obedience. *Leviticus 26:3-13*
3. Punishment for disobedience. *Leviticus 26:14-46*
4. Exhortations for Christians. *Hebrews 13:1-25*
5. Your decrees are wonderful. *Psalm 119:129-144*

A proverb: The light of the righteous rejoices, but the lamp of the wicked goes out. *Proverbs 13:9*

A prayer: We want to be obedient to your Word, O Lord. Forgive us for our disobedience. Bless our leaders. Teach us hospitality. May we always confess your name.

Day 74

The two censuses of Israel

1. The census in Sinai. *Numbers 1:1-46*
2. The census in Moab. *Numbers 26:1-51, 63-65*
(One census was made in Sinai and the other, forty years later, in Moab. You may compare the numbers of each tribe. The tribe of Levi is not included in these readings.)

A proverb: The simple are adorned with folly, but the clever are crowned with knowledge. *Proverbs 14:18*

A prayer: We thank you, Lord, that you know each one of us and that even our hairs are numbered. Help us learn to know each person in our church and to pray for each one.

Day 75

Arrangement of the camp. Census of the Levites

1. The responsibility of the Levites. *Numbers 1:47-54*
2. The arrangement of the camp. *Numbers 2:1-34*
3. The census of the Levites. *Numbers 3:1-39*
4. The census of the firstborn and the redemption money. *Numbers 3:40-51*

A proverb: The plans of the mind belong to mortals, but the answer of the tongue is from the Lord. *Proverbs 16:1*

A prayer: Lord, we thank you for calling leaders in the church. Give them strength and wisdom for their tasks. Show us how we can support them.

Day 76

Duties, census, and consecration of the Levites

1. Division of work of the three Levite families. *Numbers 4:1-33*
2. Census of eligible Levite men. *Numbers 4:34-49*
3. Census of the Levites made forty years later. *Numbers 26:57-62*
4. Purification of the Levites. *Numbers 8:5-26*
5. Tassels on the garments. *Numbers 15:37-41*

A proverb: Wisdom is at home in the mind of one who has understanding, but it is not known in the heart of fools. *Proverbs 14:33*

A prayer: We thank you, Lord, for calling administrators in the church. Bless them as they care for buildings and funds given to you and the work of your kingdom. Help us all to be responsible stewards.

Day 77

The march from Sinai to Paran

1. The silver trumpets. *Numbers 10:1-10*
2. The Israelites leave Sinai. *Numbers 10:11-36*
3. Problems in the desert. *Numbers 11:1-35*
4. The complaint of Miriam and Aaron. *Numbers 12:1-16*

A proverb: Better to be despised and have a servant, than to be self-important and lack food. *Proverbs 12:9*

A prayer: O Lord, forgive us our complaints and dissatisfaction. Teach us how to be satisfied and to trust in your presence in whatever state we are. Thank you for your guidance and protection when we travel.

Day 78

The exploration of Canaan

1. The mission of the twelve spies. *Numbers 13:1-33*
2. The rebellion of the people. *Numbers 14:1-45*
3. Moses remembers what happened. *Deuteronomy 9:22-24*
4. Death for violation of the Sabbath. *Numbers 15:32-36*

A proverb: When a land rebels it has many rulers; but with an intelligent ruler there is lasting order. *Proverbs 28:2*

A prayer: Forgive us, Lord, for our rebellion against your will and directions. Help us see the seriousness of such actions. Thank you for your mercy and your forgiveness.

Day 79

The account of the rebellion. Several new statutes

1. Moses recounts the story of the rebellion.
   Deuteronomy 1:19-46
2. Duties of the priests and Levites. *Numbers 18:1-9*
3. Offerings for priests and Levites. *Numbers 18:8-32*
4. Instructions for the water of purification.
   Numbers 19:1-22

A proverb: In the transgression of the evil there is a snare, but the righteous sing and rejoice. *Prov. 29:6*

A prayer: Help us, Lord, to give of our best to the church in tithes and offerings. Above all, help us give ourselves as a living sacrifice for your honor and glory.

Day 80

The rebellion of Korah, Dathan, and Abiram

1. The rebellion of Korah against Moses and Aaron.
   Numbers 16:1-40
2. The grumbling of the assembly. *Numbers 16:41-50*
3. Renewed vindication of Aaron. *Numbers 17:1-13*
4. The priestly blessing. *Numbers 6:22-27*
5. Stages in the journey from Sinai to Kadesh.
   Numbers 33:16-36

A proverb: The wise of heart will heed commandments, but a babbling fool will come to ruin. *Proverbs 10:8*

A prayer: Forgive us, Lord, for times when we have complained against you or against our church leaders. We want to recognize those whom you have called to your service. Help us to do our part and be satisfied with our place of service.

Day 81

The march from Kadesh to Moab

1. The feast of trumpets. *Leviticus 23:23-25; Numbers 29:1-6*
2. Moses' disobedience. *Numbers 20:1-13*
3. Edom denies Israel passage. *Numbers 20:14-21*
4. The death of Aaron. *Numbers 20:22-29; Deut. 10:6-9*
5. Defeat of the Canaanite king Arad. *Numbers 21:1-3*
6. The bronze snake. *Numbers 21:4-9*
7. Journey to Moab. *Num. 21:10-20; Deut. 2:1-23*

A proverb: Wisdom is a fountain of life to one who has it, but folly is the punishment of fools. *Proverbs 16:22*

A prayer: Thank you, Lord, for leading us through life in paths we have not known before. Teach us to recognize things to bypass and what to overcome. Bless those who lead us.

Day 82

Victory over Amorites. End of journey

1. Defeat of Sihon. *Num. 21:21-31; Deut. 2:24-37*
2. Defeat of Og, king of Bashan. *Numbers 21:32-22:1; Deuteronomy 3:1-11*
3. Stages from Kadesh to Moab. *Numbers 33:37-49*
4. Moses remembers God's providence. *Deut. 8:1-20*
5. Gratitude for what God has done. *Psalm 118:15-29*

A proverb: The memory of the righteous is a blessing, but the name of the wicked will rot. *Prov. 10:7*

A prayer: Thank you, God, for your many blessings and for victory over difficulties. You have kept us from danger and have shown us your righteousness. May you continue to guide and protect us.

Day 83

Balak and Balaam

1. Balak, king of Moab, calls Balaam. *Numbers 22:2-14*
2. Balaam summoned again. *Numbers 22:15-19*
3. Balaam goes to Moab in answer to God's voice. *Numbers 22:20-35*
4. First oracle: Israel blessed. *Numbers 22:36—23:12*
5. Second oracle: Israel blessed. *Numbers 23:13-26*
6. Third oracle: Israel blessed. *Numbers 23:27—24:14*

A proverb: A false witness will perish, but a good listener will testify successfully. *Proverbs 21:28*

A prayer: Lord, help us to be faithful witnesses to your message and purpose for all people. Forgive us when we have said only what people want to hear. Thank you for your blessing on God's people.

Day 84

Balaam's final oracle. Defeat of the Midianites

1. The prophecy of Balaam. *Numbers 24:15-25*
2. The sin of yoking with Baal of Peor. *Numbers 25:1-18*
3. The defeat of the Midianites. *Numbers 31:1-24*
4. The division of the spoils. *Numbers 31:25-54*

A proverb: Better the poor walking in integrity than one perverse of speech who is a fool. *Proverbs 19:1*

A prayer: Lord, forgive our sinfulness even after you have made such wonderful promises showing your purpose in our midst. Thank you for the Star of Jacob that has come into our lives and given us victory over evil.

Day 85

Colonization of the Transjordan

1. The proposition of Reuben and Gad. *Numbers 32:1-15*
2. The promise of Reuben and Gad. *Numbers 32:16-38*
3. The half tribe of Manasseh. *Numbers 32:39-42*
4. Moses remembers the agreement. *Deuteronomy 3:12-20*
5. The inheritance of Zelophehad. *Numbers 27:1-11*
6. Zelophehad's daughters receive their inheritance. *Numbers 36:1-13*
7. Let us worship our Maker. *Psalm 95:1-11*

A proverb: The righteousness of the upright saves them, but the treacherous are taken captive by their schemes. *Proverbs 11:16*

A prayer: We praise you, O God, that all of us, women and men, have been made heirs in Jesus Christ. Help us share your truth with all who are around us.

Day 86

Moses' exhortation in Moab

1. Introduction. *Deuteronomy 1:1-8*
2. Obedience requested of God's laws. *Deut. 4:1-14*
3. Israel was a special people. *Deuteronomy 4:20-40*
4. Wicked nations living in Canaan to be destroyed. *Deuteronomy 7:1-26*
5. Fear God and walk in his ways. *Deut. 10:12-22*

A proverb: The righteous will never be removed, but the wicked will not remain in the land. *Proverbs 10:30*

A prayer: We confess our faith in your ways, O Lord. Work in our lives and direct us as we go forward in obedience to your direction.

Day 87

Mandates regarding the conquest of Canaan

1. Introduction. *Deuteronomy 4:44-49; 3:21-22*
2. Canaanites to be driven out. *Numbers 33:50-56*
3. Boundaries for Israel in Canaan. *Numbers 34:1-12*
4. To fulfill the promise, God will drive out the enemy. *Deuteronomy 9:1-6*
5. Worship in one place, in one way. *Deut. 12:1-28*
6. Mandates regarding warfare. *Deut. 20:1-20; 24:5*

A proverb: Those who despise the word bring destruction on themselves, but those who respect the commandment will be rewarded. *Proverbs 13:13*

A prayer: We want to worship only you, O Lord. Forgive us when we have given allegiance to someone or something else. Thank you that worship can be anywhere, in spirit and in truth.

Day 88

The treatment of slaves and the poor. Philemon

1. Laws regarding Hebrew slaves. *Exodus 21:1-11*
2. Treatment and redemption of slaves. *Lev. 25:39-55*
3. Laws on the treatment of the poor and of servants. *Deuteronomy 15:1-18*
4. Those excluded from the assembly. *Deut. 23:1-8*
5. Miscellaneous laws. *Deuteronomy 23:15-25; 24:6-7*
6. Paul's letter to Philemon. *Philemon 1:1-25*

A proverb: A ruler who oppresses the poor is a beating rain that leaves no food. *Proverbs 28:3*

A prayer: Lord, forgive us for our indifference toward the poor. Teach us how to share with them and to understand their situation. May we learn of your justice, as revealed in the Bible.

Day 89

Laws regarding offerings and tithes

1. Tithes are for the Lord. *Deuteronomy 14:22-29*
2. Firstborn consecrated. *Exod. 34:19-20; Deut. 15:19-23*
3. Offerings for priests, Levites; for thanksgiving.
   Deuteronomy 18:1-8; 26:1-15
4. Supplementary offerings. *Numbers 15:1-31*
5. Blessings that come from tithing. *Malachi 3:6-12*
6. Thanksgiving for God's goodness. *Psalm 100:1-5*

A proverb: Honor the Lord with your substance and with the first fruits of all your produce; then your barns will be filled with plenty, and your vats will be bursting with wine. *Proverbs 3:9-10*

A prayer: We thank you, Lord, for the good things you give us. We honor you with our gifts and our tithes. Forgive us for our selfishness and our greed.

Day 90

Laws of legal justice

1. Judges; courts of appeal. *Deut. 16:18-20; 17:8-13*
2. Choosing a king. *Deuteronomy 17:14-20*
3. Witnesses; murder cases; various situations.
   Deuteronomy 19:15-21: 21:1-9, 10-23
4. Lawsuits among Christians. *1 Corinthians 6:1-11*
5. Seven things the Lord hates. *Proverbs 6:16-19*
6. Faithfulness to the law. *Psalm 119:81-96*

A proverb: Those who forsake the law praise the wicked, but those who keep the law struggle against them. *Proverbs 28:4*

A prayer: We honor you, Lord, for you are a just God. Help us know how to be subject to your servants who administer justice among us.

Day 91

Problems of the family and of sexual relations

1. A test for an unfaithful wife. *Numbers 5:11-31*
2. Marriage violations. *Deuteronomy 22:13-30*
3. The problem of incest in Corinth. *1 Corinthians 5:1-13*
4. Sexual immorality. *1 Corinthians 6:12-20*
5. The blessing of keeping the law. *Psalm 119:9-24*

A proverb: A wise child loves discipline, but a scoffer does not listen to rebuke. *Proverbs 13:1*

A prayer: Keep us pure, O God, that our thoughts and actions may honor you, our spouses, and our families. Forgive us for impure thoughts and actions.

Day 92

The cities of refuge

1. Purpose of the cities of refuge. *Numbers 35:9-34*
2. Instructions for these cities. *Deuteronomy 19:1-13*
3. The three cities in the Transjordan. *Deuteronomy 4:41-43*
4. The six cities of refuge. *Joshua 20:1-9*
5. The coming of a prophet. *Deuteronomy 18:15-22*
6. Hope in the Word of God. *Psalm 119:49-72*

A proverb: The Lord does not let the righteous go hungry, but he thwarts the craving of the wicked. *Proverbs 10:3*

A prayer: We thank you, Lord, that we can come to you with our burdens and our sin, to find forgiveness and rest. May your unfailing love be our refuge forever.

Day 93

The conclusion of the Law of Moses

1. Various humanitarian laws. _Deuteronomy 19:14; 24:10-22_
2. Various laws of human justice. _Deuteronomy 25:1-19_
3. The conclusion of the law. _Deuteronomy 26:16-19_
4. The naming of Joshua. _Numbers 27:12-23_
5. Moses forbidden to cross the Jordan. _Deuteronomy 3:23-29_
6. Moses' final instructions. _Deuteronomy 31:1-29_

A proverb: The teaching of the wise is a fountain of life, so that one may avoid the snares of death. _Proverbs 13:14_

A prayer: We thank you, Lord, for those who have translated and printed the Bible in many languages all over the world. We pray for our Bible teachers. Help us understand the importance of Bible reading and study.

Day 94

The consequences of disobedience

1. The altar on Mount Ebal. _Deuteronomy 27:1-10_
2. The twelve curses. _Deuteronomy 27:11-26_
3. The consequences of disobedience. _Deuteronomy 28:15-68_

A proverb: Blessings are on the head of the righteous, but the mouth of the wicked conceals violence. _Proverbs 10:6_

A prayer: We recognize the consequences of our sins, O God, but we also know that your mercy in Christ Jesus can give us pardon and new life. May your presence in our lives give us victory over sin.

Day 95

The blessing of obedience

1. The twelve blessings. *Deuteronomy 28:1-14*
2. The renewal of the covenant. *Deuteronomy 29:1-29*
3. The offer of life and death. *Deuteronomy 30:1-20*
4. Advice to a son. *Proverbs 3:21-26*
5. God's Law is light in our path. *Psalm 119:105-120*

A proverb: My child, do not forget my teaching, but let your heart keep my commandments; for length of days and years of life and abundant welfare they will give you. *Proverbs 3:1-2*

A prayer: We praise you, God, for we have found life in you through Jesus Christ. We thank you for your promises and for your blessings. Help us live in faithfulness.

Day 96

The last words of Moses

1. The song of Moses. *Deuteronomy 31:30—32:47*
2. Moses' death announced. *Deuteronomy 32:48-52*
3. The Prayer of Moses. *Psalm 90:1-17*
4. Praise to the Lord. *Psalm 117:1-2*

A proverb: All our steps are ordered by the Lord; how then can we understand our own ways? *Proverbs 20:24*

A prayer: Our lives are in your hand, O Lord. In you we have put our trust. We sing of your unfailing love. May your favor rest upon us.

Day 97

Moses blesses the tribes, then dies

1. Moses' blessing. *Deuteronomy 33:1-29*
2. The death of Moses in Moab. *Deuteronomy 34:1-12*
3. God's instructions to Joshua. *Joshua 1:1-18*
4. Praise to the Lord. *Psalm 113:1-9*

A proverb: To get wisdom is to love oneself; to keep understanding is to prosper. *Proverbs 19:8*

A prayer: We thank you, God, for your blessings and for guiding us. Make us a blessing to others. Help us be strong and courageous in the calling you have given us.

Day 98

Crossing the Jordan into Canaan

1. The sending of two spies to Jericho. *Joshua: 2:1-24*
2. The crossing of the Jordan. *Joshua 3:1-17*
3. Setting up twelve stones in Gilgal. *Joshua 4:1-24*
4. The presence of the Lord. *Psalm 114:1-8*

A proverb: Where there is no guidance, a nation falls, but in an abundance of counselors there is safety. *Proverbs 11:14*

A prayer: O Lord, we thank you for your presence when we pass through difficult experiences. Help us not to forget past experiences of your guidance. We want to celebrate your goodness and your wisdom.

Day 99

The destruction of Jericho and the sin of Achan

1. Circumcision and the Passover at Gilgal. *Joshua 5:1-12*
2. An angel meets Joshua. *Joshua 5:13-15*
3. The conquest of Jericho. *Joshua 6:1-27*
4. The sin of Achan. *Joshua 7:1-26*
5. The faith of Rahab. *Hebrews 11:30-31*

A proverb: Even in laughter the heart is sad, and the end of joy is grief. *Proverbs 14:13*

A prayer: O Lord, we confess our greed that often destroys what you want to do in our lives. May we be faithful to your Word even when we do not understand it. Thank you for bringing victory in situations that seem impossible.

Day 100

Conquest of Ai. Deception of the Gibeonites

1. The conquest of Ai. *Joshua 8:1-29*
2. The deception of the Gibeonites. *Joshua 9:1-27*
3. The defeat of the five kings of the Amorites. *Joshua 10:1-15*

A proverb: Whoever blesses a neighbor with a loud voice, rising early in the morning, will be counted as cursing. *Proverbs 27:14*

A prayer: O divine Shepherd, help us discern the true condition of people in need around us. Give us a generous heart for those unknown to us who request our help and a spirit of discernment to know how we can best help such people. May we dare to risk ourselves in performing deeds of mercy.

Day 101

Conquest of Canaan completed
1. The campaign in the south. *Joshua 10:16-43*
2. The campaign in the north. *Joshua 11:1-15*
3. A summary of the conquest. *Joshua 11:16—12:24*
4. The reading of the Law. *Joshua 8:30-35*

A proverb: Where there are no oxen, there is no grain; abundant crops come by the strength of the ox. *Proverbs 14:4*

A prayer: Thank you, Lord, for renewing your covenant with each generation. Thank you for the Bible and for those who translate it into everyday language, for everyone.

Day 102

Division of the land east of the Jordan
1. Moses' instructions. *Numbers 26:52-56; 34:13-29*
2. Land still to be taken. *Joshua 13:1-7*
3. Land east of the Jordan. *Joshua 13:8-14*
4. For Reuben. *Joshua 13:15-23; 1 Chronicles 5:1-10*
5. For Gad. *Joshua 13:24-28; 1 Chronicles 5:11-17*
6. Half tribe of Manasseh and families. *Joshua 13:29-33; 1 Chronicles 5:23-26*
7. The Lord's love endures forever. *Psalm 136:16-26*

A proverb: Those who till their land will have plenty of food, but those who follow worthless pursuits have no sense. *Proverbs 12:11*

A prayer: We praise you, Lord, because we have seen how your love endures forever. Teach us to love as you have loved us, for your honor and glory.

Day 103

The inheritance of Caleb. Ephesians, chapter 1
1. Division of land west of the Jordan. *Joshua 14:1-5*
2. Caleb chooses his inheritance. *Joshua 14:6-15*
3. The conquests of Caleb. *Joshua 15:13-19*
4. The descendants of Caleb. *1 Chronicles 2:18-55*
5. Spiritual blessings in Christ. *Ephesians 1:1-23*
6. The blessings of faithfulness. *Psalm 81:1-16*

A proverb: The reward for humility and fear of the Lord is riches and honor and life. *Proverbs 22:4*

A prayer: Thank you, O God, for adopting us as your sons and daughters and for the blessings you have given us. Thank you for your seal, the Holy Spirit, who guarantees our redemption and inheritance with your people.

Day 104

The inheritance of Judah. Ephesians, chapter 2
1. The territory of Judah. *Joshua 15:1-12*
2. The cities of Judah. *Joshua 15:20-63*
3. The descendants of Judah. *1 Chronicles 4:1-23*
4. Saved through faith. *Ephesians 2:1-10*
5. Reconciliation through the cross. *Ephesians 2:11-22*
6. Love for God's commandments. *Psalm 119:121-128*

A proverb: The good leave an inheritance to their children's children, but the sinner's wealth is laid up for the righteous. *Proverbs 13:22*

A prayer: We thank and praise you, Lord, because you have broken down barriers that divide different races. Forgive us for not breaking down barriers in our lives, in the church, and in our communities.

Day 105

Land for Ephraim and Manasseh. Ephesians 3

1. The territory of Ephraim. *Joshua 16:1-10*
2. The descendants of Ephraim. *1 Chronicles 7:20-29*
3. The territory of the tribe of Manasseh. *Josh. 17:1-18*
4. The descendants of Manasseh. *1 Chronicles 7:14-19*
5. The powerful acts of God. *Psalm 77:1-20*
6. The ministry of Paul. *Ephesians 3:1-21*

A proverb: A friend loves at all times, and kinsfolk are born to share adversity. *Proverbs 17:17*

A prayer: We praise you, Lord, because the gospel of Jesus Christ is for all people. Thank you that faithful witnesses have proclaimed the gospel even to rulers and even with suffering. May we always be faithful in our witness to all nations.

Day 106

The inheritance of Benjamin. Ephesians, chapter 4

1. Land for the seven tribes. *Joshua 18:1-10*
2. The territory of Benjamin. *Joshua 18:11-28*
3. Descendants of Benjamin. *1 Chronicles 7:6-12; 8:1-40*
4. The unity of the body of Christ. *Ephesians 4:1-16*
5. New life in Christ. *Ephesians 4:17-32*
6. Righteous living. *Psalm 101:1-8*

A proverb: Casting the lot puts an end to disputes and decides between powerful contenders. *Proverbs 18:18*

A prayer: Thank you, Lord, for those who are preparing God's people for works of service. May we all grow in unity. Forgive us for all kinds of impurity, and teach us your ways to true righteousness and holiness.

Day 107

Tribes of Simeon, Zebulun, Issachar. Ephesians 5

1. Territory and descendants of Simeon. *Joshua 19:1-9; 1 Chronicles 4:24-43*
2. The territory of Zebulun. *Joshua 19:10-16*
3. Territory and descendants of Issachar. *Joshua 19:17-23; 1 Chronicles 7:1-5*
4. God's blessings. *Psalm 103:1-22; 115:12-18*
5. The Christian walk. *Ephesians 5:1-20*

A proverb: For the wise the path of life leads upward, in order to avoid Sheol below. *Proverbs 15:24*

A prayer: May our lives, O God, reflect your light. Forgive us for foolish talk and for all obscenity. May we be filled with your Spirit and give thanks always in our hearts because of your great salvation.

Day 108

Tribes of Asher, Naphtali, Dan. Ephesians 6

1. Territory and descendants of Asher. *Joshua 19:24-31; 1 Chronicles 7:30-40*
2. Territory of Naphtali. *Joshua 19:32-39; 1 Chronicles 7:13*
3. Territory of Dan. *Joshua 19:40-48*
4. End of distribution. *Joshua 19:49-51; 21:43-45*
5. Refuge in the Lord. *Psalm 31:1-24*
6. The armor of God. *Ephesians 6:1-24*

A proverb: The righteous walk in integrity—happy are the children who follow them! *Proverbs 20:7*

A prayer: O Lord, help us treat others as you would treat them. May we take the whole armor of God so that we can withstand the devil and all his schemes. Teach us how to pray in the Spirit on all occasions.

Day 109

The descendants and the inheritance
of the tribe of Levi

1. Instructions for the Levites. *Numbers 35:1-8*
2. The descendants of Levi. *1 Chronicles 6:1-30, 50-53*
3. The cities of the Levites. *Joshua 21:1-42;*
   1 Chronicles 6:54-81

A proverb: Do not withhold good from those to
whom it is due, when it is in your power to do it.
Do not say to your neighbor, "Go, and come again,
tomorrow I will give it" —when you have it with
you. *Proverbs 3:27-28*

A prayer: We thank you, Lord, for those you have
assigned to minister to us. Teach us how to give of
our inheritance and of our substance for their
needs. Help us to be faithful in praying for our spiritual leaders and in cooperating with them.

Day 110

The return of the soldiers of the eastern tribes

1. The altar near the Jordan. *Joshua 22:1-34*
2. Joshua's farewell to the leaders. *Joshua 23:1-16*
3. Praise for the greatness of God. *Psalm 135:1-21*

A proverb: Be wise, my child, and make my heart
glad, so that I may answer whoever reproaches me.
Proverbs 27:11

A prayer: O Lord, forgive us our false assumptions
that sometimes lead to misunderstandings. Teach
us how to listen to each other, to be fair, and to be
active peacemakers among those who would treat
each other with violence for their own advantage.

Day 111

Covenant renewal. Death of Joshua

1. Covenant renewal in Shechem. *Joshua 24:1-28*
2. The death of Joshua. *Joshua 24:29-33; Judges 2:6-9*
3. Conquests completed and incomplete. *Judges 1:1-36*
4. Conquests in the Transjordan. *1 Chronicles 5:18-22*

A proverb: Where there is no prophecy, the people cast off restraint, but happy are those who keep the law. *Proverbs 29:18*

A prayer: Thank you, Lord, for symbols such as baptism, reminding us of our promises to follow you. Forgive us for any unfaithfulness. Lead us on to holiness and service.

Day 112

The apostasy of Israel and the first judges

1. The angel of the Lord. *Judges 2:1-5*
2. The cycle of apostasy in Israel. *Judges 2:10-3:6*
3. Othniel, Ehud, and Shamgar as judges. *Judges 3:7—4:3*
4. The descendants of Esau (Seir). *Genesis 36:20-30; 1 Chronicles 1:38-42*
5. The rulers of Edom. *Gen. 36:31-43; 1 Chron. 1:43-54*

A proverb: The unjust are an abomination to the righteous, but the upright are an abomination to the wicked. *Proverbs 29:27*

A prayer: O Lord, we pray today for those who have renounced their faith in you, either intentionally or because of indifference. You know them inside out. Work in their lives that they might recognize their condition and renew their faith.

Day 113

Deborah as judge

1. The victory of Deborah and Barak over the Canaanites. *Judges 4:4-24*
2. The Song of Deborah. *Judges 5:1-31*
3. The apostasy of Israel and the call of Gideon: The Lord is peace. *Judges 6:1-24*

A proverb: The eyes of the Lord keep watch over knowledge, but he overthrows the words of the faithless. *Proverbs 22:12*

A prayer: O Lord, we thank you for women who have led your people to faithfulness and to victory over Satan's power. Raise up such women among us, and help us discern their gifts and affirm their ministry.

Day 114

Gideon as judge

1. The beginning of Gideon's ministry. *Judges 6:25-40*
2. The defeat of the Midianites. *Judges 7:1-25*
3. The destruction of Zebah and Zalmunna. *Judges 8:1-21*
4. Gideon's ephod. *Judges 8:22-28*

A proverb: Righteousness guards one whose way is upright, but sin overthrows the wicked. *Proverbs 13:6*

A prayer: Teach us to trust in your power and in your wisdom, O Lord. Forgive us for putting our trust in ourselves. Deliver us from the sin of pride, from counting too much on the praise of people. Teach us humility, and show us the strength of cooperating with others in serving your purposes.

Day 115

The reign of Abimelech
1. Idolatry after Gideon's death. *Judges 8:29-35*
2. Abimelech crowned king in Shechem. *Judges 9:1-6*
3. The parable of Jotham. *Judges 9:7-21*
4. The destruction of Shechem. *Judges 9:22-49*
5. The death of Abimelech. *Judges 9:50-57*
6. Tola and Jair as judges. *Judges 10:1-5*
7. The oppression of the Ammonites. *Judges 10:6-18*

A proverb: The crooked of mind do not prosper, and the perverse of tongue fall into calamity. *Proverbs 17:20*

A prayer: O Lord, we pray for deceitful and evil persons around us. Help us make known to them the outcome of their evil ways and the hope and peace available in Jesus Christ. Guard us from putting trust in such people.

Day 116

Jephthah, Iban, Elon, and Abdon as judges
1. Jephthah defeats Ammonites. *Judges 11:1-33*
2. Jephthah's vow. *Judges 11:34-40*
3. The battle with the Ephraimites. *Judges 12:1-7*
4. Iban, Elon, and Abdon as judges. *Judges 12:8-15*
5. Birth of Samson. *Judges 13:1-25*

A proverb: It is a snare for one to say rashly, "It is holy," and begin to reflect only after making a vow. *Proverbs 20:25*

A prayer: O Lord, forgive us for making rash promises. May we be faithful to our vows. We dedicate our family and each of our lives to you. Help us to do so in a way that honors only you.

Day 117

Samson as judge

1. Samson's marriage with a woman from Timnah. *Judges 14:1-20*
2. Samson's vengeance on the Philistines. *Judges 15:1-20*
3. Samson and Delilah. *Judges 16:1-22*
4. The death of Samson. *Judges 16:23-31*

A proverb: Whoever wanders from the way of understanding will rest in the assembly of the dead. *Proverbs 21:16*

A prayer: Lord of the church, we pray for the youth of the church, that they may find their life partners among believers, those who are faithful to you. Help us experience the power of your Spirit in our lives and use that power with true wisdom.

Day 118

The Danite settlement in Laish and the priest's concubine

1. The idols and priest of Micah the Ephraimite. *Judges 17:1-13*
2. The conquest of Laish by the Danites. *Judges 18:1-31*
3. The Levite and his concubine. *Judges 19:1-30*

A proverb: The crown of the wise is their wisdom, but folly is the garland of fools. *Proverbs 14:24*

A prayer: O Lord, free us from the vicious cycle of violence, and forgive us from a desire to carry out vengeance. Help us to see and understand the result of disobeying your laws. We leave judgment in your hands. Teach us how to return good for evil.

Day 119

The problem of preserving the Benjamite tribe

1. The war of the other tribes against Benjamin. *Judges 20:1-48*
2. Women for the Benjamite survivors. *Judges 21:1-25*

A proverb: The souls of the wicked desire evil; their neighbors find no mercy in their eyes. *Proverbs 21:10*

A prayer: Free us from lawlessness, O God. We confess that our ways are not your ways. We praise you for your direction in Creation, in the church, and in our lives. Help us to seek mercy and to understand the wisdom of your laws.

Day 120

The story of Ruth

1. Ruth goes to Bethlehem with Naomi. *Ruth 1:1-22*
2. Ruth meets Boaz. *Ruth 2:1-23*
3. Boaz decides to redeem Ruth. *Ruth 3:1-18*
4. The marriage of Boaz and Ruth. *Ruth 4:1-22*

A proverb: Those who oppress the poor insult their Maker, but those who are kind to the needy honor him. *Proverbs 14:31*

A prayer: O Protector of widows and orphans, we thank you for your providential care. Thank you for those who pay their employees just wages and are kind to the poor. We also thank you for those marriages in which spouses seek to honor you and are faithful to you and to each other.

Day 121

The birth and call of Samuel

1. The birth of Samuel. *1 Samuel 1:1-28*
2. Hannah's prayer. *1 Samuel 2:1-11*
3. The wickedness of Eli's sons. *1 Samuel 2:12-26*
4. Prophecy against Eli's house. *1 Samuel 2:27-36*
5. God's call to Samuel. *1 Samuel 3:1-21*

A proverb: Even children make themselves known by their acts, by whether what they do is pure and right. *Proverbs 20:11*

A prayer: O Lord, we thank you for parents who have encouraged their sons and daughters to enter Christian service. Thank you for calling people to serve you. Help us hear your voice and respond to your call with devoted service.

Day 122

The Philistines and the ark of the covenant

1. The Philistines capture the ark. *1 Samuel 4:1-22*
2. The ark in Philistia. *1 Samuel 5:1-12*
3. The ark returned to Israel. *1 Samuel 6:1—7:1*
4. The victory over the Philistines. *1 Samuel 7:2-13*
5. Samuel as judge. *1 Samuel 7:14-17*

A proverb: The perverse get what their ways deserve, and the good, what their deeds deserve. *Proverbs 14:14*

A prayer: We thank you, O God, for faithful leaders such as Samuel who have given new life to the church through the Holy Spirit. We pray that such leaders will grow up among us, be respected and honored, and have a long and fruitful ministry.

Day 123

Saul crowned as the first king of Israel

1. Israel asks for a king. *1 Samuel 8:1-22*
2. Samuel anoints Saul. *1 Samuel 9:1—10:16*
3. Saul made king of Israel. *1 Samuel 10:17-27*
4. The genealogy of Saul. *1 Chronicles 9:35-44*

A proverb: The glory of a king is a multitude of people; without people a prince is ruined. *Proverbs 14:28*

A prayer: Forgive us, Lord, for hankering after the ways of the world and wanting to give our allegiance to someone or something other than you and your kingdom. May we find joy in following your way and accepting your reign in our lives.

Day 124

The beginning of Saul's reign and Samuel's farewell

1. Saul frees Jabesh Gilead from the Ammonites. *1 Samuel 11:1-11*
2. Saul confirmed as king. *1 Samuel 11:12-15*
3. Samuel's farewell speech. *1 Samuel 12:1-25*
4. Trust and commitment to the Lord. *Psalm 37:1-40*

A proverb: The fear of the Lord prolongs life, but the years of the wicked will be short. *Proverbs 10:27*

A prayer: Help us live in obedience to you, O King of kings, and in subjection to those who rule over us, cooperating as far as conscience allows. Forgive us for rebelling against your Word and your will. We know that your laws are wise and true and that your punishment is just. May we serve you faithfully.

Day 125

The war with the Philistines

1. Saul's impatience to fight. *1 Samuel 13:1-15*
2. Israel's lack of weapons. *1 Samuel 13:16-22*
3. Jonathan's victory over the Philistines. *1 Samuel 13:23—14:23*
4. Jonathan and Saul's curse. *1 Samuel 14:24-46*
5. War against other enemies. *1 Samuel 14:47-52*

A proverb: A wise king winnows the wicked, and drives the wheel over them. *Proverbs 20:26*

A prayer: O Lord, give us patience in seeking your guidance. Forgive us for making unwise promises. May we find only in you the arms we need to defeat Satan in our lives and communities.

Day 126

God rejects Saul as king and chooses David

1. The victory over the Amalekites. *1 Samuel 15:1-9*
2. Saul's disobedience. *1 Samuel 15:10-35*
3. Samuel anoints David. *1 Samuel 16:1-13*
4. David plays his harp for Saul. *1 Samuel 16:14-23*
5. A new song for the Lord. *Psalm 149:1-9*
6. A psalm of praise and thanksgiving. *Psalm 145:1-21*

A proverb: The sacrifice of the wicked is an abomination to the Lord, but the prayer of the upright is his delight. *Proverbs 15:8*

A prayer: Lord, forgive us when we think we know better than you. We rejoice with our sisters and brothers in singing your praises. We glorify you every day because you are gracious, you are faithful, and you are righteous. May our mouths always give honor to your name.

Day 127

David defeats Goliath, meets Jonathan

1. Goliath challenges Saul's army. *1 Samuel 17:1-11*
2. David defeats Goliath. *1 Samuel 17:12-58*
3. David's friendship with Jonathan and Saul's jealousy. *1 Samuel 18:1-9*
4. David's praise of the Lord. *Psalm 144:1-15*

A proverb: The house of the wicked is destroyed, but the tent of the upright flourishes. *Proverbs 14:11*

A prayer: O Lord, thank you for the joy of friendship. Grant us faith to do great and difficult things in your name. Give us a humble spirit in the time of victory so that we can recognize your power and your mighty acts rather than glorifying ourselves.

Day 128

Jonathan helps David escape Saul's wrath

1. Saul fears David, tries to kill him. *1 Samuel 18:10-30*
2. Jonathan and Michal save David from Saul's wrath. *1 Samuel 19:1-24*
3. The covenant between Jonathan and David. *1 Samuel 20:1-23*
4. A cry for help. *Psalm 143:1-12*

A proverb: Some friends play at friendship but a true friend sticks closer than one's nearest kin. *Proverbs 18:24*

A prayer: O Friend of the friendless, help us be friends with those who are treated unjustly. May we not be afraid to defend their cause. Give us wisdom in seeking their freedom without using violence or dishonest methods.

Day 129

David flees from Saul

1. Jonathan helps David escape. *1 Samuel 20:24-42*
2. The priest Ahimelech helps David. *1 Samuel 21:1-9*
3. David in Gath, Adullam, and Mizpah. *1 Samuel 21:10—22:5*
4. The prayer of David in Gath. *Psalm 56:1-13*
5. Saul kills the priests of Nob. *1 Samuel 22:6-23*
6. The psalm David wrote when he heard the news. *Psalm 52:1-9*

A proverb: Fools show their anger at once, but the prudent ignore an insult. *Proverbs 12:16*

A prayer: Lord, we pray for those who are being persecuted unjustly. Give them faithfulness, patience, and wisdom to know how they should act. Grant us wisdom in relating to violent people.

Day 130

David spares Saul's life in a cave in En-gedi

1. David in Keilah and Ziph. *1 Samuel 23:1-18*
2. The treachery of the Ziphites. *1 Samuel 23:19-29*
3. A prayer of David when in Ziph. *Psalm 54:1-7*
4. David spares Saul's life in En-gedi. *1 Samuel 24:1-22*
5. A prayer of David written in the cave. *Psalm 57:1-11*
6. A psalm of David concerning Saul. *Psalm 7:1-17*

A proverb: Crooked minds are an abomination to the Lord, but those of blameless ways are his delight. *Proverbs 11:20*

A prayer: Lord, give us respect for the lives of our enemies or those who treat us with disdain. Forgive us when we think evil just because others are doing evil against us. Teach us your way of peace.

Day 131

The marriage of David with Abigail

1. Nabal refuses to help David. *1 Samuel 25:1-13*
2. Abigail appeases David. *1 Samuel 25:14-35*
3. David marries Abigail. *1 Samuel 25:36-44*
4. David asks for deliverance. *Psalm 59:1-17*
5. A psalm asking for protection. *Psalm 140:1-13*
6. Another psalm written in the cave. *Psalm 142:1-7*

A proverb: The wicked put on a bold face, but the upright give thought to their ways. *Proverbs 21:29*

A prayer: O God of peace, thank you for people who are peacemakers. Help us know the satisfaction of helping others in need. We pray for organizations that seek to feed those suffering from hunger.

Day 132

David spares Saul's life again, then flees

1. David again spares Saul's life, this time in Ziph. *1 Samuel 26:1-25*
2. David promises to obey God's law. *Ps. 119:145-160*
3. David flees to Gath of the Philistines. *1 Samuel 27:1—28:2*
4. Philistines mistrust David. *1 Samuel 29:1-11*
5. David's call to the Lord. *Psalm 141:1-10*

A proverb: One who walks in integrity will be safe, but whoever follows crooked ways will fall into the Pit. *Proverbs 28:18*

A prayer: Forgive us, Lord, when we have not respected those appointed to serve you. Teach us to honor them even when we disagree with them. We pray that you might give our leaders wisdom and understanding.

Day 133

Warriors join David

1. Israelites join David in Ziklag. *1 Chronicles 12:1-22*
2. The three chiefs in David's band. *2 Samuel 23:8-17; 1 Chronicles 11:10-19*
3. David's thirty chiefs. *2 Samuel 23:18-39; 1 Chronicles 11:20-47*
4. David's call to the Lord. *Psalm 28:1-9*

A proverb: Iron sharpens iron, and one person sharpens the wits of another. *Proverbs 27:17*

A prayer: May we be brave for you, O Lord. Take away any fears of the unknown, and any dread of the powers of Satan. May the greater power of your Spirit guide and accompany us in the battle with evil. You, O Lord, are the strength of your people.

Day 134

David and the Amalekites

1. David goes after the Amalekites. *1 Samuel 30:1-15*
2. David defeats the Amalekites and distributes the spoils. *1 Samuel 30:16-31*
3. David's psalm of thanksgiving for deliverance. *Psalm 18:1-50*
4. A plea for mercy. *Psalm 123:1-4*

A proverb: Happy is the one who is never without fear, but one who is hard-hearted will fall into calamity. *Proverbs 28:14*

A prayer: O Lord, may the awareness of your presence ever be real in our lives, that we might know your protection and deliverance. May we come to you daily in prayer and supplication. We praise and honor you for your love.

Day 135

The end of Saul's reign

1. Saul and the witch of Endor. *1 Samuel 28:3-25*
2. Israelites defeated; death of Saul and his sons.
   1 Samuel 31:1-13; 1 Chronicles 10:1-14
3. David receives the news. *2 Samuel 1:1-16*
4. David's lament. *2 Samuel 1:17-27*

A proverb: The wise are cautious and turn away from evil, but the fool throws off restraint and is careless. *Proverbs 14:16*

A prayer: We put our trust in you, O Lord. Forgive us when we have tried to know the future through mediums, fortunetellers, horoscopes, astrology, or the like. Guard us against darkness in our midst.

Day 136

David made king of Judah

1. David anointed king over Judah. *2 Samuel 2:1-7*
2. War between the house of Saul and the house of David. *2 Samuel 2:8—3:1*
3. The genealogy of David. *1 Chronicles 2:3-17*
4. The family of David. *2 Samuel 3:2-5; 1 Chron. 3:1-4*
5. A prayer of vindication over enemies. *Ps. 35:1-28*
6. An evening prayer. *Psalm 4:1-8*

A proverb: Loyalty and faithfulness preserve the king, and his throne is upheld by righteousness. *Proverbs 20:28*

A prayer: O Lord, we want to speak of your righteousness and praise you all day long. We also desire the vindication of your people when they are mocked and persecuted. Give us love for our enemies, and show us how to deal with them.

Day 137

The death of Abner and of Ish-bosheth

1. The agreement between David and Abner.
   2 Samuel 3:6-21
2. Joab murders Abner. *2 Samuel 3:22-39*
3. The death of Ish-bosheth. *2 Samuel 4:1-12*
4. A cry for vengeance. *Psalm 109:1-31*

A proverb: Scoundrels concoct evil, and their speech is like a scorching fire. *Proverbs 16:27*

A prayer: Lord, forgive us when we have returned evil for good. Teach us how to overcome evil with good. Help us see how violence breeds violence. Teach us your love.

Day 138

David proclaimed king over all Israel

1. David is made king of all Israel, conquers Jerusalem, and makes it his capital. King Hiram of Tyre helps him build his palace. David's family grows. David defeats Philistines. *2 Samuel 5:1-25*
2. Parallel story. *1 Chronicles 3:5-9; 11:1-9; 12:23-40; 14:1-17*
3. David expresses confidence in God. *Psalm 63:1-11; Psalm 119:73-80*

A proverb: Many seek the favor of a ruler, but it is from the Lord that one gets justice. *Proverbs 29:26*

A prayer: We also thirst for you, O God. Day and night we remember your salvation, and in our churches we gather to praise you and proclaim your Word. We trust in your presence and in your direction for our lives. We sing for joy in the shadow of your wings.

Day 139

David brings the ark to Jerusalem

1. While David is bringing the ark to Jerusalem, Uzzah steadies it with his hand and dies. The ark is left at the house of Obed-edom. Later it is carried in a more proper way to the city of David amidst great rejoicing and feasting. *2 Samuel 6:1-19; 1 Chronicles 13:1-14; 15:1—16:3*
2. Michal's criticism of David. *2 Samuel 6:20-23*
3. David's prayer for peace. *Psalm 122:1-9*
4. A psalm of blessing and peace. *Psalm 128:1-6*

A proverb: A cheerful heart is a good medicine, but a downcast spirit dries up the bones. *Proverbs 17:22*

A prayer: O Lord, may there be peace in our homes, our towns, and our cities. Help us be channels for bringing your peace and well-being to those swallowed up by crime, violence, and hatred.

Day 140

The first worship service in Jerusalem. Psalm 106

1. Asaph and his helpers. *1 Chronicles 16:4-6*
2. David's psalm of thanksgiving. *1 Chronicles 16:7-36*
3. Levites minister in Jerusalem and in Gibeon. *1 Chronicles 16:37-43*
4. God's care and Israel's rebellion. *Psalm 106:1-48*

A proverb: No wisdom, no understanding, no counsel, can avail against the Lord. *Proverbs 21:30*

A prayer: May the worship in our churches give glory to you, O Lord. We pray that our worship and song leaders may be inspired and led by the Holy Spirit. We confess our sins of the past and consecrate our lives to you.

Day 141

God's promise to David

1. David desires to build a house for the ark, but God says no. David responds with praise and humble recognition of God's greatness. He accepts God's promise to bless his offspring. *2 Samuel 7:1-29; 1 Chronicles 17:1-27*
2. David asks for God's direction and blessing. *Psalm 25:1-22*
3. A psalm of praise. *Psalm 96:1-13*

A proverb: It is an abomination to kings to do evil, for the throne is established by righteousness. *Proverbs 16:12*

A prayer: We know, O Lord, that our requests to you reflect our human understanding. Thank you for answering our prayers according to your wisdom. You know what is best for us. Teach us how to pray and how to discern your Spirit among us.

Day 142

The expansion of David's kingdom

1. David extends his kingdom by subduing nations around him. *2 Samuel 8:1-14; 10:1-19; 1 Chronicles 18:1-13; 19:1-19*
2. A psalm asking for God's help. *Psalm 60:1-12*

A proverb: A servant who deals wisely has the king's favor, but his wrath falls on one who acts shamefully. *Proverbs 14:35*

A prayer: O Lord, we ask for your aid in our struggle against the evil around us and our sinful nature within. Forgive us when we try to act alone. May we depend on the power of the Holy Spirit.

Day 143

David's kindness shown to Mephibosheth

1. David's officials. *2 Sam. 8:15-18; 1 Chron. 18:14-17*
2. David's kindness to Mephibosheth. *2 Samuel 9:1-13*
3. God's faithfulness and discipline to Israel from the exodus till the time of David. *Psalm 78:1-72*

A proverb: Whoever diligently seeks good seeks favor, but evil comes to the one who searches for it. *Proverbs 11:27*

A prayer: We praise you, O God, for your mercy and goodness working in our lives, even when we disobeyed you. We promise to tell the children the stories of your glorious deeds, so they can tell the coming generations to set their hope in you.

Day 144

The adultery of David

1. David tries to cover up. *2 Samuel 11:1-27*
2. Nathan reveals to David the nature of his sin. *2 Samuel 12:1-25*
3. David's psalm of confession and forgiveness. *Psalm 51:1-19*
4. Joab's victory over Ammonites. *2 Samuel 12:26-31; 1 Chronicles 20:1-3*

A proverb: Surely there is no one on earth so righteous as to do good without ever sinning. *Ecclesiastes 7:20*

A prayer: We recognize that we can not hide our sins from you, Lord, since you see everything. We confess our sexual sins, whether in thought or in action, and ask forgiveness for them. Just as we trust in your forgiveness, so help us to forgive others.

Day 145

Troubles in David's family
1. Amnon rapes his sister Tamar. *2 Samuel 13:1-21*
2. Absalom kills his brother Amnon. *2 Samuel 13:22-39*
3. Absolom returns to Jerusalem. *2 Samuel 14:1-24*
4. A plea for mercy. *Psalm 41:1-13*

A proverb: The righteous hate falsehood, but the wicked act shamefully and disgracefully. *Proverbs 13:5*

A prayer: Lord, we pray for families where there is suffering because of sin and hatred. May the power of Christ and his pardon bring peace to them. Help us know how to relate to them and bring healing. Give us hope to share even in situations that seem hopeless to human eyes.

Day 146

The conspiracy of Absalom
1. Absalom's arrogance. *2 Samuel 14:25-33*
2. Absalom's conspiracy in Hebron. *2 Samuel 15:1-12*
3. Three psalms of supplication to God. *Psalm 17:1-15; Psalm 55:1-23; Psalm 94:1-23*

A proverb: Foolish children are a grief to their father and bitterness to her who bore them. *Proverbs 17:25*

A prayer: Lord, we thank you that in time of distress, when everyone seems against us, we can come to you with confidence and find hope in you. We pray for those who are depressed and hopeless, that they might find hope in you.

Day 147

David flees from Jerusalem with anguish

1. David decides to leave Jerusalem. *2 Sam. 15:13-37*
2. The lie of Ziba and the curse of Shimei. *2 Samuel 16:1-14*
3. David pleads for mercy. *Psalm 6:1-10*
4. A cry of anguish. *Psalm 22:1-31*

A proverb: It is not right to be partial to the guilty, or to subvert the innocent in judgment. *Proverbs 18:5*

A prayer: May your presence, Lord, give us peace and understanding when others lie about us or curse us. Forgive us when we have acted unjustly or mean toward others. Help us bring comfort to those who suffer injustice.

Day 148

Absalom enters Jerusalem. David flees

1. Absalom in Jerusalem. *2 Samuel 16:15-23*
2. Absalom accepts the advice of Hushai. *2 Samuel 17:1-23*
3. David flees to Mahanaim. *2 Samuel 17:24-29*
4. Several prayers of David. *Psalm 13:1-6; Psalm 20:1-9; Psalm 61:1-8; Psalm 70:1-5*
5. A psalm of vindication over the enemy. *Psalm 74:1-23*

A proverb: A glad heart makes a cheerful countenance, but by sorrow of heart the spirit is broken. *Proverbs 15:13*

A prayer: Lord, we thank you for those who are ready to help us when we are in distress or in a difficult situation. Make us aware of how we can help others who are without family or friends.

Day 149

Battle between Absalom's army and David's army

1. David's confidence in God. *Psalm 3:1-8*
2. Refuge in the Lord. *Psalm 71:1-24*
3. The battle in the forest of Ephraim. *2 Samuel 18:1-8*
4. Joab kills Absalom. *2 Samuel 18:9-18*
5. David mourns the death of Absalom. *2 Samuel 18:19—19:8*

A proverb: An ally offended is stronger than a city; such quarreling is like the bars of a castle. *Prov. 18:19*

A prayer: O God, we pray for those who are grieving the loss of a family member. Show us how to be present with them in a consoling and encouraging way.

Day 150

David returns to Jerusalem

1. The elders of Judah ask David to return. *2 Samuel 19:9-15*
2. Restored relations with Shimei and Ziba. *2 Samuel 19:16-30*
3. David returns to Jerusalem. *2 Samuel 19:31-43*
4. The rebellion of Sheba. *2 Samuel 20:1-26*
5. David rejoices in the Lord. *Psalm 21:1-13*

A proverb: A person's pride will bring humiliation, but one who is lowly in spirit will obtain honor. *Proverbs 29:25*

A prayer: Lord, teach us to be kind to those who have treated us unkindly. Help us see the foolishness of rebellion and of war because of an offense. Guide us so that we can make peace between those who are offended with each other.

Day 151

Other happenings in the latter days of David

1. David's dealings with the house of Saul. *2 Samuel 21:1-14*
2. Victory over giants of the Philistines. *2 Samuel 21:15-22; 1 Chronicles 20:4-8*
3. David's song of praise. *2 Samuel 22:1-51*

A proverb: The horse is made ready for the day of battle, but the victory belongs to the Lord. *Proverbs 21:31*

A prayer: We thank you, Lord, for your faithfulness in keeping your promises. We praise you because you are perfect in all your ways. We kneel before you in recognition of your great mercy and salvation. Work in our lives for your glory.

Day 152

David's census of his fighting men

1. David decides to take a census of his fighting men. Joab tries to dissuade him. God is angry because of this and punishes David. David builds an altar to God, and the plague is stopped. *2 Samuel 24:1-25; 1 Chronicles 21:1—22:1*
2. A prayer of confession. *Psalm 38:1-22*

A proverb: All one's ways may be pure in one's own eyes, but the Lord weighs the spirit. *Proverbs 16:2*

A prayer: You know our hearts, O Lord. Forgive us when our motives have been twisted by selfishness or jealousy. Examine our hearts, show us any evil within, and cleanse us. Do not forsake us. Make haste to help us, O Lord, our salvation, so we can know your truth and your justice.

Day 153

The rebellion of Adonijah and the anointing of Solomon

1. Adonijah tries to become king. *1 Kings 1:1-10*
2. Bathsheba and Nathan intervene. *1 Kings 1:11-27*
3. David makes Solomon king. *1 Kings 1:28-53*
4. David declares his integrity. *Psalm 26:1-12*
5. A prayer of Solomon. *Psalm 72:1-20*

A proverb: A king who sits on the throne of judgment winnows all evil with his eyes. *Proverbs 20:8*

A prayer: O Lord, we pray for our rulers that they may govern with justice. Free them from evil and corruption. We ask you to guide them that our countries may live in peace with each other and that peoples within our countries may learn to accept and respect each other.

Day 154

David's instructions to Solomon

1. Preparations for the construction of the temple. *1 Chronicles 22:2-19*
2. Instructions for the Levites. *1 Chronicles 23:1-32*
3. A list of the temple musicians. *1 Chronicles 6:31-49*
4. A prayer of an afflicted man when he is faint. *Psalm 102:1-28*

A proverb: Plans are established by taking advice; wage war by following wise guidance. *Proverbs 20:18*

A prayer: O God, we pray for those planning to raise a new church building. Give them guidance so that it may honor you rather than human pride. Thank you for those who have gifts of architecture and construction.

Day 155

Priests, singers, gatekeepers, treasurer, judges
1. Divisions of the priests. *1 Chronicles 24:1-31*
2. Divisions of the singers. *1 Chronicles 25:1-31*
3. Divisions of the gatekeepers. *1 Chron. 26:1-19*
4. Treasurers and the judges. *1 Chronicles 26:20-32*

A proverb: Anyone who tends a fig tree will eat its fruit, and anyone who takes care of a master will be honored. *Proverbs 27:18*

A prayer: Lord of the church, we pray for pastors, deacons, and elders with responsibilities in our churches. May your Spirit be with them and guide them. Help us receive the tasks that you have given each one of us.

Day 156

David's government. Plans for the temple
1. Army divisions. *1 Chronicles 27:1-15*
2. Officers of the tribes. *1 Chronicles 27:16-24*
3. The king's overseers. *1 Chronicles 27:25-34*
4. David's plans for the temple. *1 Chronicles 28:1-21*
5. Offerings for the temple. *1 Chronicles 29:1-9*
6. David's prayer; Solomon acknowledged as king. *1 Chronicles 29:10-25*

A proverb: Righteous lips are the delight of a king, and he loves those who speak what is right. *Proverbs 16:13*

A prayer: We thank you, Lord, for people who give willingly for the work of the church. Bless those who administer these offerings so that they can work honestly and for your honor. Help us to administer our belongings well.

Day 157

The death of David. Solomon's reign begins

1. The last words of David. *2 Samuel 23:1-7*
2. David's charge to Solomon. *1 Kings 2:1-9*
3. David's death. *1 Kings 2:10-12; 1 Chronicles 29:26-30*
4. Solomon, Adonijah, and Abiathar. *1 Kings 2:13-27*
5. Joab and Shimei killed. *1 Kings 2:28-46*
6. A psalm of David about the wicked. *Psalm 5:1-12*

A proverb: The dread anger of a king is like the growling of a lion; anyone who provokes him to anger forfeits life itself. *Proverbs 20:2*

A prayer: Lord, we pray for those who suffer the wrath of rulers. Protect us. May we be subject to rulers except when this conflicts with our loyalty to God. Help us to do right, show love to all, and overcome evil with good.

Day 158

Solomon's song of love. Christ's love

1. The first scene. *Song of Songs (Sol.) 1:1—2:7*
2. The second scene. *Song of Songs 2:8—3:5*
3. The third scene. *Song of Songs 3:6—5:1*
4. Christ's love for the church compared with marriage. *Ephesians 5:21-33*

A proverb: What is desirable in a person is loyalty, and it is better to be poor than a liar. *Proverbs 19:22*

A prayer: Thank you, Lord, for love found in marriage. Help anyone married to grow in that love and be faithful to the spouse. Thank you for Christ's love for the church. May believers be faithful to that love.

Day 159

Solomon's love song completed. The wedding

1. Dreams of the bride; of the groom. *Song of Songs 5:2—6:3; 6:4—7:9*
2. Mutual love. *Song of Songs 7:10—8:14*
3. Solomon's marriage. *1 Kings 3:1-2*
4. A wedding song. *Psalm 45:1-17*
5. Christ's new commandment. *John 15:12-17*

A proverb: Many proclaim themselves loyal, but who can find one worthy of trust? *Proverbs 20:6*

A prayer: O God, we pray that those recently married may find joy and satisfaction in their mutual love. Help the church to support married couples in faithfulness to their vows.

Day 160

Solomon's government. His request for wisdom

1. Solomon's officials; his daily provisions. *1 Kings 4:1-19; 4:20-28*
2. Solomon's request for wisdom. *1 Kings 3:3-15; 2 Chronicles 1:1-13*
3. Solomon's wisdom shown. *1 Kings 3:16-28; 4:29-34*
4. The purpose of wisdom. *Proverbs 1:1-6*
5. Two kinds of wisdom. *James 3:13-18*

A proverb: The fear of the Lord is the beginning of knowledge; fools despise wisdom and instruction. *Proverbs 1:7*

A prayer: Lord, give us wisdom that comes from heaven so that we may be pure, peace-loving, considerate, submissive, full of mercy and good fruit, impartial, and sincere. Forgive us for depending too much on human wisdom.

Day 161

Descriptions of wisdom
1. The benefits of wisdom. *Proverbs 1:20—2:22*
2. Wisdom is supreme. *Proverbs 4:1-27*
3. The excellence of wisdom. *Proverbs 8:1-36*

A proverb: A wise child makes a glad father, but a foolish child is a mother's grief. *Proverbs 10:1*

A prayer: O Lord, give us insight and discretion that we may know your truth and walk in it. Enlighten us as we study your Word. Help us to learn from our parents and from those who have gone before us.

Day 162

Proverbs regarding our lips, tongue, and speech
1. The house of wisdom. *Proverbs 9:1-12*
2. Speaking. *Proverbs 10:11, 14, 18-19, 21, 31-32; 11:12; 12:6, 13, 18, 22; 13:2-3; 14:3, 7; 15:1-2, 4, 7, 28; 16:23, 30; 17:4, 28; 18:6-7, 20-21; 19:28; 21:6, 23; 28:23; 29:20; Ecclesiastes 7:21-22*
3. Truth. *Proverbs 18:17; 20:14; 28:21; 29:24.* False witness. *12:17; 14:5; 19:5, 9*
4. Quarreling. *Proverbs 17:14, 19; 22:10*
5. Taming the tongue. *James 3:1-12*
6. Evil speaking condemned. *Psalm 50:1-23*

A proverb: One who forgives an affront fosters friendship, but one who dwells on disputes will alienate a friend. *Proverbs 17:9*

A prayer: O Lord, teach us how to tame our tongue. Forgive us for speaking evil and untruths. May we bless our neighbors and not belittle them. Give us understanding to discern the true and righteous.

Day 163

Common themes in the proverbs of Solomon

1. Discipline. *Proverbs 10:17; 12:1; 13:18, 24; 15:5, 32; 19:18; 22:15; 29:15, 17*
2. The rich and the poor. *Proverbs 10:15; 13:7; 14:20; 18:23; 19:4, 7; 21:5, 13, 17, 20; 22:7, 16; 28:8, 22*
3. Putting up security. *6:1-5; 11:15; 17:18; 20:16; 27:13*
4. The lazy. *Proverbs 6:6-11; 10:4-5, 26; 12:27; 13:4; 15:19; 18:9; 19:15, 24; 20:4, 13; 21:25; 22:13*
5. Gossip. *Proverbs 11:13; 16:28; 18:8; 20:19*
6. Fools. *Proverbs 6:12-15; 10:10; 11:29; 13:20; 17:16, 21; 19:10; 27:3; Ecclesiastes 7:1-6*
7. Pride. *Proverbs 13:10; 15:25; 16:18; 21:24; 27:2*
8. The quick-tempered. *Proverbs 14:17, 29; 15:18; 16:32; 19:19; 29:22; Ecclesiastes 7:9*
9. A quarrelsome wife. *Prov. 19:13; 21:9, 19; 27:15-16*
10. Bribes. *Prov. 17:8, 23; 18:16; 19:6; 21:14; Eccl. 7:7*

A proverb: A slave pampered from childhood will come to a bad end. *Proverbs 29:21*

A prayer: Forgive us, Lord, for being quick-tempered. May your Spirit help us control our anger.

Day 164

Sayings of the wise

1. Prohibitions and teachings. *Prov. 22:17—24:22*
2. Other sayings of the wise. *Prov. 24:23-34; 27:23-27*
3. The search for wisdom. *Ecclesiastes 7:13-18, 23-25*

A proverb: The righteous know the needs of their animals, but the mercy of the wicked is cruel. *Proverbs 12:10*

A prayer: Lord, help us be aware of the dangers of alcohol. Forgive us for abuse of drugs or alcohol.

Day 165

The construction of the temple

1. Hiram, king of Tyre, brings materials and artisans to construct the Jerusalem temple, three stories high, with stones shaped at the quarry. The sanctuary is lined with gold; wings of cherubs reach from wall to wall. *1 Kings 5:1-6:36; 2 Chronicles 2:1—3:14*

A proverb: The hand of the diligent will rule, while the lazy will be put to forced labor. *Proverbs 12:24*

A prayer: We thank you, Lord, for artisans who can make beautiful work with wood, stone, or metal. Help us also to see the beauty in your Creation. May our works of art be for your honor and glory.

Day 166

Solomon's palace and the temple's furnishings

1. Details of Solomon's palace. *1 Kings 7:1-12*
2. The two bronze pillars, the sea of bronze, the ten wash basins with their stands, other utensils, furniture of gold. *1 Kings 7:13-51; 2 Chronicles 3:15—4:22*
3. The work completed. *1 Kings 6:37-38; 2 Chronicles 5:1*

A proverb: There is gold, and abundance of costly stones; but the lips informed by knowledge are a precious jewel. *Proverbs 20:15*

A prayer: O Lord, make us be aware that luxurious homes and church buildings do not always honor you. Forgive us whenever they have led us to pride and to a confusion of values in our private life and in the life of the church.

Day 167

Dedication of the temple

1. The tribes gather. Levites bring the ark into the temple. The glory of the Lord fills the temple. Solomon tells the people he has carried out the promise of God to David. Then he praises God, showing this to be a house where all can pray. *1 Kings 8:1-30; 2 Chronicles 5:2—6:21*

2. A prayer psalm, possibly from when the temple was dedicated. *Psalm 132:1-18*

A proverb: If a king judges the poor with equity, his throne will be established forever. *Proverbs 29:14*

A prayer: O Lord God, may our church buildings be truly houses of prayer. Teach us how to pray when we are together and when we are alone. May prayer become a more important part of our worship services.

Day 168

Solomon's prayer and God's response

1. Solomon prays for God to forgive the people when they confess their sin. He asks God to listen to their prayers. Solomon blesses the people. Sacrifices and burnt offerings are made, and a holy festival is observed for seven days. *1 Kings 8:31-66; 2 Chronicles 6:22—7:10*

A proverb: The eyes of the Lord are in every place, keeping watch on the evil and the good. *Prov. 15:3*

A prayer: We praise you, Lord, because we know that we can come before you with confidence; you will hear our prayer. Thank you for your mercy. Help us confess our sins to you and to others.

Day 169

God's covenant; Solomon's government

1. God's covenant with Solomon. *1 Kings 9:1-9; 2 Chronicles 7:11-22*
2. Solomon's building program, his sacrifices as a king, his merchant fleet. *1 Kings 9:10-28; 2 Chronicles 8:1-18*
3. The glory and beauty of Jerusalem. *Psalm 48:1-14*
4. A song of ascents. *Psalm 127:1-5*

A proverb: An estate quickly acquired in the beginning will not be blessed in the end. *Proverbs 20:21*

A prayer: Lord, help us understand that the carrying out of your promises depends upon our faithfulness to you. Forgive us when we have forsaken your teachings. May our lives reflect your love.

Day 170

The queen of Sheba visits. Solomon's splendor

1. The queen of Sheba visits Solomon. *1 Kings 10:1-13; 2 Chronicles 9:1-12*
2. Solomon's trading in horses and chariots. *2 Chronicles 1:14-17*
3. Solomon's abundance and splendor. *1 Kings 10:14-29; 2 Chronicles 9:13-28*
4. The danger of riches. *Luke 12:13-21*
5. A treasure in heaven. *Luke 12:22-34*

A proverb: Anyone who robs father or mother and says, "That is no crime," is partner to a thug. *Proverbs 28:24*

A prayer: O Lord, forgive us for giving so much effort to laying up earthly treasures. Help us hold true values and lay up treasure in heaven.

Day 171

The failure of anxious toil

1. Everything, even wisdom, is vexation. *Eccl. 1:1-18*
2. Chasing after wind. *Ecclesiastes 2:1-26*
3. There is a time for everything. *Ecclesiastes 3:1-8*
4. Enjoy work; God is Judge. *Ecclesiastes 3:9-22*
5. Injustices of life. Have awe for God. *Ecclesiastes 4:1-16; 5:1-7*

A proverb: Better is the end of a thing than its beginning; the patient in spirit are better than the proud in spirit. *Ecclesiastes 7:8*

A prayer: We stand in awe before you, O God. Forgive us for our words and promises that we cannot fulfill. Many things in life seem to be folly, yet in you we find true meaning for life. We praise and honor you with all of our life.

Day 172

The deceit of riches

1. Riches are dangerous. *Ecclesiastes 5:8—6:12*
2. False trust in riches. *Psalm 49:1-20*
3. The destiny of the wicked. *Psalm 73:1-28*
4. Favoritism. Oppression. *James 2:1-13; 5:1-6*
5. About wealth. *Proverbs 11:4, 26, 28; 16:16*

A proverb: A good name is to be chosen rather than great riches, and favor is better than silver or gold. *Proverbs 22:1*

A prayer: Keep us, Lord, from putting our trust in riches. Instead, help us put our trust in you. We confess that the attractions of this world often engulf and blind us. Give us wisdom to keep our values in proper perspective.

Day 173

The conclusion of the Teacher

1. Realities that cannot be understood. *Eccl. 8:2-17*
2. A common destiny for all. *Ecclesiastes 9:1-12*
3. Wisdom is better than folly. *Eccl. 9:13—10:20*
4. Advice for the young and the old. *Eccl. 11:1—12:8*
5. Conclusion; what the Teacher found. *Ecclesiastes 12:9-14; 7:27-29*

A proverb: Wisdom gives strength to the wise more than ten rulers that are in a city. *Ecclesiastes 7:19*

A prayer: O Lord, guide us in our search for wisdom. Above all we want to fear you and keep your commandments. Help us know what is good and what is evil. We praise you that Jesus Christ has given meaning to our lives.

Day 174

Warnings against adultery. A noble wife

1. Solomon's many wives. *1 Kings 11:1-8*
2. Warning against adultery. *Proverbs 5:1-23; 6:20-35*
3. Warning against the adulteress. *Prov. 7:1-27; 9:13-18*
4. Other proverbs about adultery. *Proverbs 22:14; 29:3; Ecclesiastes 7:26*
5. The noble wife. *Proverbs 31:10-31*

A proverb: A good wife is the crown of her husband, but she who brings shame is like rottenness in his bones. *Proverbs 12:4*

A prayer: Creator God, we confess that relations between men and women are often not right. Teach us how to have healthy relations between men and women, between husbands and wives.

Day 175

The downfall of Solomon

1. God's punishment of Solomon. *1 Kings 11:9-25*
2. Jeroboam's rebellion against Solomon. *1 Kings 11:26-40*
3. The death of Solomon. *1 Kings 11:41-43; 2 Chronicles 9:29-31*
4. The psalm of Ethan the Ezrahite. *Psalm 89:1-52*

A proverb: By justice a king gives stability to the land, but one who makes heavy exactions ruins it. *Proverbs 29:4*

A prayer: O Lord, our hearts grieve to see how sin can destroy a nation or a family. Reveal to us any beginning of disobedience in our lives. Show us your way of repentance and new life in Christ.

Day 176

The division of the kingdom

1. All Israel goes to Shechem to crown Rehoboam. He says he will oppress the people more than Solomon. Ten tribes rebel, led by Jeroboam. *1 Kings 12:1-24; 2 Chronicles 10:1—11:4*
2. Reign of Rehoboam in Judah. *2 Chronicles 11:5-23*
3. Jeroboam reigns from Shechem, starts sinful worship. *1 Kings 12:25-33*
4. The justice of God. *Psalm 75:1-10*

A proverb: If a ruler listens to falsehood, all his officials will be wicked. *Proverbs 29:12*

A prayer: Lord, we pray for countries where rulers oppress the people. Work in their midst to bring justice and understanding. May the Christians living there be instruments of reconciliation and peace.

Day 177

The apostasy of Israel and of Judah

1. The prophecy of the man of God. *1 Kings 13:1-10*
2. The death of the man of God. *1 Kings 13:11-32*
3. Jeroboam's idolatry and the judgment of God.
   1 Kings 13:33—14:20
4. The apostasy of Rehoboam. *1 Kings 14:21-24*
5. War with Shishak, king of Egypt. *1 Kings 14:25-28; 2 Chronicles 12:1-12*

A proverb: Like a roaring lion or a charging bear is a wicked ruler over a poor people. *Proverbs 28:15*

A prayer: Help us understand your leading in our lives. Forgive us when we have persisted in our own ways and not in the truth of your Word. Direct us through all difficulties and temptations.

Day 178

Death of Rehoboam. Abijah and Asa reign

1. Rehoboam dies. His son Abijah continues in idolatry, is attacked by Jeroboam, and is victorious. His son Asa removes idols from Judah, is attacked by Cush, and is victorious. *1 Kings 14:29—15:15; 2 Chronicles 12:13—14:15*
2. Asa's reform. *2 Chronicles 15:1-19*

A proverb: The integrity of the upright guides them, but the crookedness of the treacherous destroys them. *Proverbs 11:3*

A prayer: Forgive us for any duplicity and hypocrisy. You know the condition of our hearts. Help us live and act in such a way that we can be honest with those around us. Let the integrity of our lives give witness to your love.

Day 179

Nadab, Baasa, Elah, Zimri, Omri, Ahab

1. The reign of Nadab and the revolt of Baasa.
   1 Kings 15:25-34
2. Civil war between Baasa and Asa. *1 Kings
   15:16-24; 2 Chronicles 16:1-14*
3. The prophecy of Jehu. *1 Kings 16:1-7*
4. The revolt and reign of Zimri. *1 Kings 16:8-20*
5. Omri and his son Ahab. *1 Kings 16:21-34*
6. Elijah announces a drought. *1 Kings 17:1-7*
7. A psalm asking for help. *Psalm 12:1-8*

A proverb: Those who are kind reward themselves, but the cruel do themselves harm. *Proverbs 11:17*

A prayer: Lord, teach us to be kind to those around us. May our expressions of kindness be a reflection of your love. Forgive us for our self-centeredness.

Day 180

Elijah and the prophets of Baal

1. Elijah and the widow of Zarephath. *1 Kings
   17:8-24*
2. Elijah's encounter with Obadiah and Ahab.
   1 Kings 18:1-19
3. Elijah confronts the prophets of Baal. *1 Kings
   18:20-46*
4. Elijah flees from Jezebel to Horeb. *1 Kings 19:1-18*

A proverb: If the righteous are repaid on earth, how much more the wicked and the sinner! *Proverbs 11:31*

A prayer: We praise you, O God, for showing your power in wind, rain, storms, and earthquakes. Your power is greater than any efforts of Satan. Help us also to hear the gentle whisper of your voice.

Day 181

War between Israel and Aram (Syria)
1. Elijah calls Elisha. *1 Kings 19:19-21*
2. Ahab versus Ben-hadad. *1 Kings 20:1-34*
3. A prophet condemns Ahab. *1 Kings 20:35-43*
4. Ahab steals Naboth's vineyard. *1 Kings 21:1-16*
5. The prophecy of Elijah against Ahab and Jezebel.
   1 Kings 21:17-29

A proverb: Those who are greedy for unjust gain make trouble for their households, but those who hate bribes will live. *Proverbs 15:27*

A prayer: Forgive us, Lord, for our greed and for the dishonest ways we sometimes use to get what we want. May we learn to be satisfied with what we have and share with the needy.

Day 182

Jehoshaphat in alliance with Ahab
1. The reign of Jehoshaphat in Judah. *1 Kings 22:41-44; 2 Chronicles 17:1-19; 20:31-33*
2. Jehoshaphat allies with Ahab, king of Israel, to fight Ben-hadad. The false prophets of Ahab announce victory for the coalition, but the prophet Micaiah says all Israel will be scattered and Ahab killed. *1 Kings 22:1-28: 2 Chronicles 18:1-27*

A proverb: In the light of a king's face there is life, and his favor is like the clouds that bring the spring rain. *Proverbs 16:15*

A prayer: We thank you, Lord, for women and men who have taught us the Bible. We pray for the teachers and leaders who are prophetic voices for the church through their teaching ministry.

Day 183

Ahab's death. Victories of Jehoshaphat

1. Ahab dies in Ramoth-gilead. *1 Kings 22:29-40; 2 Chronicles 18:28—19:3*
2. The reforms of Jehoshaphat. *2 Chronicles 19:4-11*
3. Jehoshaphat conquers Moabites, Ammonites, Edomites. *2 Chronicles 20:1-30*
4. The end of Jehoshaphat's reign. *1 Kings 22:45-50; 2 Chronicles 20:34-37*
5. A cry for help and for salvation. *Psalm 108:1-13*

A proverb: A king's wrath is a messenger of death, and whoever is wise will appease it. *Proverbs 16:14*

A prayer: O Lord, help us be like Jehoshaphat and like Paul by singing when we are in trouble. May the power of your Spirit give us strength and confidence at such times.

Day 184

The reigns of Ahaziah and Jehoram, kings of Israel

1. The reign and foolishness of Ahaziah. *1 Kings 22:51—2 Kings 1:18*
2. Elijah taken up into heaven; Elisha's first miracles. *2 Kings 2:1-25*
3. Jehoram allies with Jehoshaphat to put down a revolt of the Moabites. *2 Kings 3:1-27*
4. A prayer for victory over the enemy. *Psalm 129:1-8*

A proverb: Whoever is kind to the poor lends to the Lord, and will be repaid in full. *Proverbs 19:17*

A prayer: O Lord, thank you for prophets of God who inspire us. May your Spirit dwell upon others who take their places. Help them give leadership to the church and be prophetic voices to the nations.

Day 185

Elisha, the widow's son, Naaman, and the Aramean raiders

1. The Shunammite widow's son restored to life. *2 Kings 4:1-37*
2. The healing of Naaman. *2 Kings 5:1-19*
3. The greed of Gehazi, the servant of Elisha. *2 Kings 5:20-27*
4. Elisha traps and then frees the Arameans. *2 Kings 6:8-23*

A proverb: A tranquil mind gives life to the flesh, but passion makes the bones rot. *Proverbs 14:30*

A prayer: Help us, Lord, accept the simple solutions that you give us and be faithful to your laws. Forgive us for insisting on our own ways. Thank you for providing peaceful solutions for conflicts.

Day 186

Miracles of Elisha. The siege of Samaria

1. Several miracles of Elisha. *2 Kings 4:38-44; 6:1-7*
2. The siege of Samaria. *2 Kings 6:24—7:2*
3. The four lepers at end of siege. *2 Kings 7:3-20*
4. The Shunammite's land restored. *2 Kings 8:1-6*
5. Hazael, king of Aram (Syria). *2 Kings 8:7-15*
6. The wicked; God's love. *Psalm 36:1-12*

A proverb: Thorns and snares are in the way of the perverse; the cautious will keep far from them. *Proverbs 22:5*

A prayer: We praise you, Lord, for your wonderful ways and that you continue to work miracles in our time. Give us faith to trust in your promises. Forgive us for our unbelief.

Day 187

Kings of Judah: Jehoram, Ahaziah.
Kings of Israel: J(eh)oram, Jehu
1. Jehoram kills brothers, is attacked, dies of disease. His son Ahaziah is made king and is unfaithful to God; he allies with J(eh)oram against Aram. *2 Kings 8:16-29; 2 Chron. 21:1—22:6*
2. Jehu anointed king of Israel. *2 Kings 9:1-13*
3. Jehu kills J(eh)oram and Ahaziah. *2 Kings 9:14-29; 2 Chronicles 22:7-9*
4. Death of Jezebel. *2 Kings 9:30-37*

A proverb: If someone is burdened with the blood of another, let that killer be a fugitive until death; let no one offer assistance. *Proverbs 28:17*

A prayer: It pains us, Lord, to see so much violence around us. Deliver us from media that offer violence as entertainment.

Day 188

Jehu purges Israel. Reign of Athaliah in Judah
1. Jehu destroys Ahab's family. *2 Kings 10:1-17*
2. The destruction of Baal worship. *2 Kings 10:18-36*
3. Athaliah, mother of Jehoram and Ahaziah, rules over Judah. She kills her grandsons, except Joash, hidden. When seven, he is crowned king. *2 Kings 11:1-12; 2 Chronicles 22:10—23:11*
4. The reign and power of God. *Psalm 97:1-12*

A proverb: Misfortune pursues sinners, but prosperity rewards the righteous. *Proverbs 13:21*

A prayer: Thank you, O God, for people who have been faithful in spite of adverse situations. Thank you for leaders who confront evil rulers.

Day 189

Joash reigns in Judah, Jehoahaz in Israel

1. Joash is crowned. Athaliah is killed. Jehoiada the priest tutors Joash, who repairs the temple. Joash kills Zechariah the priest for denouncing him. Under attack, Joash gives temple treasures to Hazael, king of Aram. His own officials assassinate him. _2 Kings 11:13—12:21; 2 Chronicles 23:12—24:27_
2. Jehoahaz, king of Israel. _2 Kings 13:1-9_

A proverb: The human mind may devise many plans, but it is the purpose of the Lord that will be established. _Proverbs 19:21_

A prayer: Thank you, Lord, for religious leaders who are faithful to your Word. Raise up good political leaders and give guidance to them.

Day 190

Jehoash, Jeroboam in Israel; Amaziah in Judah

1. Reign of Jehoash. _2 Kings 13:10-13, 22-25_
2. Death of Elisha. _2 Kings 13:14-21_
3. Reign of Amaziah. _2 Kings 14:1-22; 2 Chron. 25:1-28_
4. Reign of Jeroboam II in Israel. _2 Kings 14:23-29_

A proverb: A king's anger is like the growling of a lion, but his favor is like dew on the grass. _Proverbs 19:12_

A prayer: We pray, O King of kings and Lord of lords, for the rulers of our nations. Work in their lives and in their decisions to bring about fairness, justice, and mercy. We pray for peace between nations, especially where kin are fighting kin. May your church be a means of reconciliation.

Day 191

The prophet Jonah. The reign of Azariah in Judah

1. The disobedience of Jonah. *Jonah 1:1-17*
2. Jonah prays, obeys God, and preaches to Nineveh. *Jonah 2:1—3:10*
3. Jonah's anger at the Lord's compassion. *Jonah 4:1-11*
4. Azariah (Uzziah), king of Judah. *2 Kings 15:1-7; 2 Chronicles 26:1-23*

A proverb: Righteousness exalts a nation, but sin is a reproach to any people. *Proverbs 14:34*

A prayer: Forgive us for our pride, O Lord, especially when it distorts our service to you. Teach us the meaning of true humility when we are before you and before those around us. May we first of all seek your reign and your righteousness.

Day 192

The prophet Amos in the time of Jeroboam II

1. Judgment on Israel's neighbors. *Amos 1:1-2:5*
2. Judgment on Israel. *Amos 2:6-16*
3. Witnesses against Israel. *Amos 3:1-15*
4. Israel has not returned to God. *Amos 4:1-13*
5. A lament and a call to repentance. *Amos 5:1-27*

A proverb: Better is a little with righteousness than large income with injustice. *Proverbs 16:8*

A prayer: We want to do good, O Lord. Forgive us when we trample on the poor or turn justice into bitterness. Help us see how our society and our living standards may bring suffering on other people. Guide us in finding ways to work for fairness, starting in our local area.

Day 193

Prophecies of Hosea and Amos against Israel

1. The sin and ruin of Ephraim. _Hosea 12:7—13:16_
2. Woe to the complacent. _Amos 6:1-14_
3. Figures of the coming judgment. _Amos 7:1-9_
4. Amos and Amaziah, priest of Bethel. _Amos 7:10-17_
5. The coming destruction of Israel. _Amos 8:1—9:10_
6. The coming restoration of Israel. _Amos 9:11-15_

A proverb: The faithful will abound with blessings, but one who is in a hurry to be rich will not go unpunished. _Proverbs 28:20_

A prayer: O Lord, we recognize your sovereignty in our lives. You know our sin and weakness. But we praise you for assurance of salvation in Jesus Christ. Thank you for restored lives.

Day 194

The adultery of Israel

1. The marriage of Hosea with Gomer. _Hosea 1:1—2:1_
2. Israel's punishment, restoration. _Hosea 2:2-23_
3. Hosea's reconciliation with his wife. _Hosea 3:1-5_
4. The unfaithfulness of Israel. _Hosea 4:1-19_
5. Judgment against Israel and Judah. _Hosea 5:1—6:3_
6. God's love for Israel. _Hosea 11:1-11_

A proverb: The field of the poor may yield much food, but it is swept away through injustice. _Proverbs 13:23_

A prayer: Thank you, God, for your deep love for us, and for sending your Son, Jesus Christ, to save us and the world. May we learn to love as you have loved us. Forgive us when our expression of love to you is two-faced.

Day 195

Hosea announces punishment, repentance, and blessings

1. The unfaithfulness of Israel. *Hosea 6:4—7:16*
2. The punishment that God will send. *Hosea 8:1-14*
3. Punishment for Israel. *Hosea 9:1—10:15*
4. The judgment of Israel and Judah for their sins. *Hosea 11:12—12:6*
5. A call to repentance. *Hosea 14:1-9*

A proverb: Bread gained by deceit is sweet, but afterward the mouth will be full of gravel. *Proverbs 20:17*

A prayer: We thank you for your forgiveness, Lord. We know that your way is right and the world's way is sin. May we walk in your righteousness and not stumble.

Day 196

The last kings of Israel. The vision of Isaiah

1. The last kings of Israel. *2 Kings 15:8-31*
2. The reign of Jotham, king of Judah. *2 Kings 15:32-38; 2 Chronicles 27:1-9*
3. The call and commission of Isaiah. *Isaiah 6:1-13*
4. The song of the vineyard and the seven woes. *Isaiah 5:1-30*

A proverb: Fine speech is not becoming to a fool; still less is false speech to a ruler. *Proverbs 17:7*

A prayer: We have heard your call in our lives, Lord. We have also found that many do not want to listen to your words. May your presence sanctify our lives that we might carry out your calling no matter what the response.

Day 197

Isaiah announces punishment on Judah

1. God reasons with a rebellious nation. *Isaiah 1:1-31*
2. A call to repentance. *Isaiah 2:1-22*
3. Ahaz, king of Judah, practices idolatry, is attacked by Israel and allied nations, who take captives to Samaria. The prophet Oded denounces them; they let captives return. Ahaz seeks help from Tiglath-pileser of Assyria, who captures Damascus. *2 Kings 16:1-9; 2 Chronicles 28:1-21*

A proverb: Whoever flatters a neighbor is spreading a net for the neighbor's feet. *Proverbs 29:5*

A prayer: Forgive us, Lord, for our blindness to things that hinder our prayers and our fellowship with you. We thank you for your promises that have been fulfilled and for those that are being fulfilled.

Day 198

Micah's prophecy against Samaria and Jerusalem

1. Judgment and mourning for Israel and Judah. *Micah 1:1-16*
2. The nature of Israel's rebellion. *Micah 2:1-13*
3. Leaders and prophets rebuked. *Micah 3:1-12*
4. The Lord's case against Israel. *Micah 6:1-16*
5. The promise of divine restoration. *Micah 4:1—5:15*

A proverb: Those who despise their neighbors are sinners, but happy are those who are kind to the poor. *Proverbs 14:21*

A prayer: Lord, teach us what it means to act justly, to love mercy, and to walk humbly with you. Help us find ways to do these things so that they might be a witness of your love and your salvation.

Day 199

Judgment coming on Jerusalem and Samaria
1. Isaiah's prophecy against Ahaz. *Isaiah 7:1-25*
2. Assyria as an instrument of God. *Isaiah 8:1-22*
3. The anger of the Lord against Israel. *Isa. 9:8—10:4*
4. The judgment of Jerusalem and Judah. *Isaiah 3:1—4:1*

A proverb: It is better to be of a lowly spirit among the poor than to divide the spoil with the proud. *Proverbs 16:19*

A prayer: O Lord, help us learn from the experience of Israel and other nations that sought their help in human leaders rather than in God. May we put our trust in you and in your promises. We praise you for Jesus, whom you sent into this world to bring us salvation.

Day 200

Prophecies against the enemies of Israel
1. A prophecy against the Philistines. *Isaiah 14:28-32*
2. A prophecy against Moab. *Isaiah 15:1—16:14*
3. A prophecy against Damascus. *Isaiah 17:1-14*
4. A prophecy against Cush (the upper Nile region). *Isaiah 18:1-7*
5. A prophecy against Egypt. *Isaiah 19:1—20:6*

A proverb: No one finds security by wickedness, but the root of the righteous will never be moved. *Proverbs 12:3*

A prayer: We know, Lord, that you see the wickedness in all nations. Give us patience to wait for your judgment on the nations. Above all, help us know your righteousness and live in your ways.

Day 201

The sin of Ahaz and the unfaithfulness of Judah

1. King Ahaz's altar and his idolatry. *2 Kings 16:10-20; 2 Chronicles 28:22-27*
2. Woes upon Ephraim and Judah. *Isaiah 28:1-29*
3. A prophecy about Jerusalem. *Isaiah 22:1-25*
4. Woe upon an obstinate nation. *Isaiah 30:1-14*

A proverb: Wine is a mocker, strong drink a brawler, and whoever is led astray by it is not wise. *Proverbs 20:1*

A prayer: Lord, help us in our worship. We want to adore you alone. Forgive us when we have given worth to other people or things that should be reserved for you. May all of our lives be for your honor and give glory to your name.

Day 202

The reign and the reform of king Hezekiah

1. The repair and purification of the temple. *2 Chronicles 29:1-36*
2. Hezekiah celebrates the Passover. *2 Chronicles 30:1—31:1*
3. A prayer asking forgiveness. *Psalm 130:1-8*

A proverb: Whoever is steadfast in righteousness will live, but whoever pursues evil will die. *Proverbs 11:19*

A prayer: We wait for you, O Lord, trusting in your forgiveness and your mercy. May we sanctify our lives for your service. Let our offerings be acceptable before you. Guide us as we unite with fellow Christians to remember your mighty deeds and your great salvation.

Day 203

The faithfulness of Hezekiah. The fall of Samaria

1. The Levites reorganized. *2 Chronicles 31:2-21*
2. A summary of King Hezekiah's reign. *2 Kings 18:1-8*
3. The reign of Hoshea and the fall of Samaria. *2 Kings 17:1-6; 18:9-12*
4. The cause of the captivity. *2 Kings 17:7-23*
5. The origin of the Samaritans. *2 Kings 17:24-41*

A proverb: The Righteous One observes the house of the wicked; he casts the wicked down to ruin. *Proverbs 21:12*

A prayer: Lord, forgive us when we are stiff-necked and let the world twist our understanding of your Word. In both discipline and blessings, show your will for our lives and for the life of your church.

Day 204

Micah and Isaiah: salvation of a remnant

1. Confession and hope. *Micah 7:1-20*
2. God's judgment on Assyria. *Isaiah 10:5-19*
3. A remnant will return. *Isaiah 10:20-34; 11:10-16*
4. A song of praise. *Isaiah 12:1-6*
5. Distress and help for Zion. *Isaiah 33:1-24*

A proverb: When justice is done, it is a joy to the righteous, but dismay to evildoers. *Proverbs 21:15*

A prayer: We thank you, Lord, for the promise that you will restore your people. We leave in your hands the judgment coming upon evil designs and the evil one. With Isaiah, we want to sing your praises and exalt your name. Thank you for the wells of salvation that give us life and hope.

Day 205

Punishment and restoration for Tyre and for Jerusalem

1. A prophecy about Tyre; destruction and restoration. *Isaiah 23:1-18*
2. Universal destruction and recognition of God. *Isaiah 24:1-23*
3. A song of praise to the Lord. *Isaiah 25:1-12*
4. A song of praise for Judah. *Isaiah 26:1-21*
5. Punishment and deliverance for Israel. *Isa. 27:1-13*

A proverb: The wicked flee when no one pursues, but the righteous are as bold as a lion. *Proverbs 28:1*

A prayer: We too can say that we have trusted in you, O God, and that you have saved us. Thank you for your mercy and pardon. May we open the gates of our lives that you may establish peace for us.

Day 206

Prophecies against Jerusalem

1. Woes upon David's city. *Isaiah 29:1-24*
2. Promise of salvation to a repentant nation. *Isaiah 30:15-33*
3. Woe to those who rely on Egypt. *Isaiah 31:1-9*
4. Warnings and hope for Jerusalem. *Isaiah 32:1-20*
5. The branch of the Lord. *Isaiah 4:2-6*

A proverb: When the wicked prevail, people go into hiding; but when they perish, the righteous increase. *Proverbs 28:28*

A prayer: We thank you, Lord, for your presence in our lives, both night and day, and for your Holy Spirit, who gives us refuge and a hiding place from the storms of life.

Day 207

The invasion of Sennacherib

1. The new Assyrian king, Sennacherib, invades Judah and takes Lachish. His commander threatens Jerusalem. Three accounts of this blasphemous challenge. *Isaiah 36:1-22; 2 Kings 18:13-37; 2 Chronicles 32:1-19*

2. A prayer for deliverance. *Psalm 64:1-10*

A proverb: Before destruction one's heart is haughty, but humility goes before honor. *Proverbs 18:12*

A prayer: O Lord, we pray for your guidance and protection in times of great danger. May we be faithful to you in spite of our fear. We thank you for saving your people from those who blaspheme your name and make fun of your purposes.

Day 208

Hezekiah asks God for help

1. Hezekiah hears of the Assyrian blasphemy and threat. Isaiah tells leaders of Judah not to fear; Sennacherib will withdraw. By letter, Sennacherib warns Hezekiah not to trust in his God. Hezekiah goes to the temple to pray, asking God for deliverance. *2 Kings 19:1-19: Isaiah 37:1-20*

2. A prayer of David requesting salvation. *Ps. 69:1-36*

A proverb: The way of the Lord is a stronghold for the upright, but destruction for evildoers. *Prov. 10:29*

A prayer: Lord, we pray for those who blaspheme your name, that you may so work in their lives that they will come to recognize your greatness and your salvation. Forgive us when we have made wrongful use of your name.

Day 209

God's response to Hezekiah through Isaiah

1. Isaiah sends message to Hezekiah, about Sennacherib. He gives Hezekiah a sign for a time of peace. The Assyrians will not enter Jerusalem. That night many Assyrians die. Sennacherib withdraws and is assassinated. *2 Kings 19:20-37; Isaiah 37:21-38; 2 Chronicles 32:20-23*
2. David requests deliverance. *Psalm 68:1-35*

A proverb: The Lord's curse is on the house of the wicked, but he blesses the abode of the righteous. Toward the scorners he is scornful, but to the humble he shows favor. *Proverbs 3:33-34*

A prayer: We thank you, God, for your great salvation, and for your power over those who plot evil. Put in our hearts a compassion for such schemers, who entrap themselves. May we share with them the hope we have in Jesus Christ.

Day 210

Proverbs collected in the time of Hezekiah

1. Practical advice; comparisons using the word *like*. *Proverbs 25:1—26:27*
2. The sayings of Agur. *Proverbs 30:1-33*
3. The sayings of King Lemuel. *Proverbs 31:1-9*

A proverb: A lying tongue hates its victims, and a flattering mouth works ruin. *Proverbs 26:28*

A prayer: Lord, forgive us for lies we have told and for flattering words meant only to bring honor to ourselves. Teach us how to honor others with our words and how to be witnesses of your truth.

Day 211

The latter years of Hezekiah
1. Hezekiah's sickness. *2 Kings 20:1-11; 2 Chronicles 32:24-26; Isaiah 38:1-8*
2. Hezekiah's psalm. *Isaiah 38:9-22*
3. Hezekiah and the king of Babylon. *Isaiah 39:1-8; 2 Kings 20:12-21; 2 Chronicles 32:27-33*
4. A psalm of praise for God's justice. *Psalm 9:1-20*

A proverb: The clever see danger and hide; but the simple go on, and suffer for it. *Proverbs 22:3*

A prayer: Thank you, Lord, for health and answering our prayers for healing. Teach us how to pray in such times, and give us faith in your promises. Help us to be ready to pray for others who are sick.

Day 212

Prophecies about Babylon and other nations
1. An oracle concerning Assyria. *Isaiah 14:24-27*
2. An oracle concerning Babylon. *Isaiah 13:1-22*
3. A taunt against Babylon. *Isaiah 14:1-23*
4. Isaiah announces the fall of Babylon. *Isaiah 21:1-10*
5. Oracles concerning Edom and Arabia. *Isa. 21:11-17*
6. Judgment against the nations. *Isaiah 34:1-17*

A proverb: Evil people seek only rebellion, but a cruel messenger will be sent against them. *Proverbs 17:11*

A prayer: When we see the evil and wars of the nations, we long for your righteous kingdom, O Lord. May our lives even now be a foretaste of your way of holiness. We praise you for our redemption and for the joy you have given us through Christ Jesus.

Day 213

Kings of Judah: Manasseh, Amon, and Josiah

1. Manasseh reigns for 55 years but does evil. His son Amon reigns the same way for 2 years and is assassinated. Josiah is a good king. In the 18th year of his reign, he has the temple repaired. *2 Kings 21:1—22:7; 2 Chron. 33:1—34:13*
2. A yearning to be in the temple. *Psalm 84:1-12*

A proverb: Folly is a joy to one who has no sense, but a person of understanding walks straight ahead. *Proverbs 15:21*

A prayer: We too desire to be in your presence, O Lord. Guide us so that in our planning we can always unite with others in worship and fellowship. Thank you for churches and worship leaders who make this possible.

Day 214

Jeremiah during time of Josiah

1. Jeremiah's call. *Jeremiah 1:1-19*
2. The apostasy of Israel. *Jeremiah 2:1-19*
3. The causes of Israel's punishment. *Jer. 2:20—3:5*
4. The faithless example of the Northern Kingdom (Samaria). *Jeremiah 3:6—4:2*

A proverb: Those who mock the poor insult their Maker; those who are glad at calamity will not go unpunished. *Proverbs 17:5*

A prayer: Thank you, God, for calling us to return to you when we have sought evil ways. Thank you for spiritual leaders like Jeremiah who have called us to you and have been faithful to your Word. Forgive our waywardness.

Day 215

Zephaniah prophesies in days of Josiah

1. God's judgment upon Judah. *Zephaniah 1:1—2:3*
2. God's judgment upon the nations. *Zephaniah 2:4-15*
3. God's punishment and restoration of Jerusalem. *Zephaniah 3:1-13*
4. The book of the Law discovered in the temple. *2 Kings 22:8-20; 2 Chronicles 34:14-28*

A proverb: The purposes in the human mind are like deep water, but the intelligent will draw them out. *Proverbs 20:5*

A prayer: Thank you, God, for purifying our lips. Thank you for rescuing the lame and gathering those who have been scattered. May we honor and praise your name among all nations.

Day 216

The reforms of King Josiah

1. Josiah has the Law read to all the people and renews the covenant. Places of idol worship are destroyed. Passover celebrated. Josiah goes out to confront Neco, king of Egypt, is wounded, and dies. Neco was going to join Assyria against the Babylonians, who had destroyed Nineveh in 612 B.C. *2 Kings 23:1-30; 2 Chronicles 34:29—5:27*

A proverb: Those who mislead the upright into evil ways will fall into pits of their own making, but the blameless will have a goodly inheritance. *Prov. 28:10*

A prayer: Give us discernment, Lord, to find in your Word instruction for our lives. May we recognize our own unfaithfulness and confess it before you. Help us renew our covenant promise made to you.

Day 217

The prophecy of Nahum; the reign of Jehoahaz

1. The Lord's anger against Nineveh. *Nahum 1:1-15*
2. The siege and fall of Nineveh. *Nahum 2:1-13*
3. Why Nineveh fell. *Nahum 3:1-19*
4. The reign of Jehoahaz. *2 Kings 23:31-35;*
   2 Chronicles 36:1-4
5. A cry to God for liberation. *Psalm 44:1-26*

A proverb: Wrath is cruel, anger is overwhelming, but who is able to stand before jealously? *Prov. 27:4*

A prayer: You are a great and mighty God, a God of justice and of mercy. May your mercy and justice reign in our lives and in the life of your church. Thank you for being slow to anger and mighty in redemption. We confess that our lives depend upon your steadfast love.

Day 218

Punishment for an unfaithful people

1. Disaster will come from the north. *Jeremiah 4:3-31*
2. Punishment for a rebellious people. *Jer. 5:1-31*
3. Jerusalem will be put under siege. *Jeremiah 6:1-30*

A proverb: Haughty eyes and a proud heart—the lamp of the wicked—are sin. *Proverbs 21:4*

A prayer: Lord, forgive our stubborn and rebellious hearts when we have lost our fear of you and have doubted your Word. Bring healing and redemption into our lives instead of punishment and death. We praise you for Jesus Christ, who gives us life eternal.

Day 219

Causes of God's coming judgment upon Judah

1. A false religion and disobedience. *Jeremiah 7:1-29*
2. Idolatry. *Jeremiah 7:30—8:3*
3. Lack of repentance. *Jeremiah 8:4-22*
4. Lack of faith and truth. *Jeremiah 9:1-24*

A proverb: Those who trust in their own wits are fools; but those who walk in wisdom come through safely. *Proverbs 28:26*

A prayer: Forgive us, Lord, for our boasting about worldly things. We want to boast only in the Lord. We praise you for your kindness, your justice, and your righteousness. Teach us to know you so that we may proclaim your character and deeds.

Day 220

More causes of God's coming judgment

1. Imitating the idolatry of other nations. *Jeremiah 9:25—10:25*
2. Breaking the covenant. *Jeremiah 11:1-17*
3. The plot against Jeremiah. *Jeremiah 11:18-23*
4. The wicked who prosper. *Jeremiah 12:1-17*
5. The parables of the linen belt and the wineskins. *Jeremiah 13:1-14*

A proverb: The wicked earn no real gain, but those who sow righteousness get a true reward. *Prov. 11:18*

A prayer: Forgive us, Lord, for following customs and traditions that are not in your will. Guard us from trusting in ritual rather than in you, from thinking that sacrifices are a substitute for obedience. We want to be faithful to our covenant with you. Deliver us from all hypocrisy.

Day 221

Jeremiah announces the captivity of Judah

1. A warning to Judah. *Jeremiah 13:15-27*
2. The parable of the drought. *Jeremiah 14:1-22*
3. Punishment by death, sword, starvation, and captivity. *Jeremiah 15:1-21*
4. The sign of celibacy. *Jeremiah 16:1-21*

A proverb: Whoever sows injustice will reap calamity, and the rod of anger will fail. *Proverbs 22:8*

A prayer: Thank you, God, for teaching us your power and your might. May we trust in you. We accept your punishment because of our sins, and we thank you for your pardon and redemption.

Day 222

Jeremiah suffers persecution for his prophecies

1. Judah will lose its inheritance. *Jeremiah 17:1-18*
2. The importance of keeping the Sabbath. *Jeremiah 17:19-27*
3. The sign of the potter. *Jeremiah 18:1-23*
4. The sign of the broken clay jar. *Jeremiah 19:1-15*
5. Jeremiah prophesies against Pashhur. *Jeremiah 20:1-6*
6. The justice of God. *Psalm 11:1-7*

A proverb: The thoughts of the righteous are just; the advice of the wicked is treacherous. *Proverbs 12:5*

A prayer: We honor you for your promises, whether blessings or punishment, because we know that you are a just God. We also praise you because you have listened to penitent sinners just as you have punished the unfaithful. May we learn from your justice.

Day 223

Jeremiah's arrest. Habakkuk's questions

1. The reign of king Jehoiakim. *2 Kings 23:36-37*
2. Jeremiah arrested and threatened with death. *Jeremiah 26:1-24*
3. Habakkuk's first question and God's answer. *Habakkuk 1:1-11*
4. Habakkuk's second question and God's answer. *Habakkuk 1:12—2:20*
5. Habakkuk's prayer. *Habakkuk 3:1-19*

A proverb: The evil do not understand justice, but those who seek the Lord understand it completely. *Proverbs 28:5*

A prayer: O Lord, we too are concerned about the corruption, violence and drunkenness around us. Help us live by faith and wait patiently on you. Keep us from complacency, and guide us in our search for justice. We rejoice in your salvation.

Day 224

Jeremiah in the time of king Jehoiakim

1. Jeremiah: 70 years of captivity. *Jeremiah 25:1-14*
2. The sign of the cup of wine. *Jeremiah 25:15-38*
3. Jehoiakim burns Jeremiah's scroll. *Jeremiah 36:1-32*
4. God's message to Baruch the scribe. *Jer. 45:1-5*

A proverb: Evil will not depart from the house of one who returns evil for good. *Proverbs 17:13*

A prayer: Many have tried to destroy your Word, O Lord, but have not succeeded. We thank you that your might is greater than theirs. Thank you for those who have preserved, translated, and taught the Bible in spite of danger to their lives.

Day 225

Messages from God for Egypt, Philistia, and Moab

The new king of Babylon, Nebuchadnezzar, defeated the Egyptians at Carchemish in Syria in 605 B.C., and then headed south to subdue other nations.

1. A message concerning Egypt. *Jeremiah 46:1-28*
2. A message concerning Philistia. *Jeremiah 47:1-7*
3. A message concerning Moab. *Jeremiah 48:1-47*

A proverb: When the wicked are in authority, transgression increases, but the righteous will look upon their downfall. *Proverbs 29:16*

A prayer: May we not be lax in doing your will, O Lord. Thank you for your Holy Spirit, who guides us and works in us. Empower us, lead us, and make us bold as witnesses to all nations that you are the Most High over all the earth.

Day 226

The Recabites, Jehoiakim, Jehoiachin, and the first captivity

1. The faithfulness of the Recabites. *Jeremiah 35:1-19*
2. Jehoiakim's end. *2 Kings 24:1-7; 2 Chronicles 36:5-8*
3. Jeremiah's prophecy about the kings of Judah. *Jeremiah 22:1-30*
4. Jehoiachin and the first captivity. *2 Kings 24:8-17; 2 Chronicles 36:9-10*
5. A psalm requesting vindication. *Psalm 43:1-5*

A proverb: The wicked is a ransom for the righteous, and the faithless for the upright. *Proverbs 21:18*

A prayer: May we be humble in the presence of your messengers, O God. Forgive us when we have stiffened our necks and hardened our hearts.

Day 227

Daniel, Zedekiah, and messages for the nations

1. Daniel and his three friends. *Daniel 1:1-21*
2. The sign of the figs. *Jeremiah 24:1-10*
3. Zedekiah's reign. *Jeremiah 52:1-3; 2 Kings 24:18-20; 2 Chronicles 36:11-16*
4. A list of the kings of Judah. *1 Chronicles 3:10-16*
5. Messages for Ammon and Edom. *Jeremiah 49:1-22*
6. Messages for Damascus, Kedar, and Hazor. *Jeremiah 49:23-33*

A proverb: When the righteous are in authority, the people rejoice; but when the wicked rule, the people groan. *Proverbs 29:2*

A prayer: O Lord, we see many nations that put confidence in military strength and violence. Show us how to put our confidence in your strength, your Word, and your reign over all nations.

Day 228

Prophesies for Elam, Zedekiah, and false prophets

1. A message for Elam. *Jeremiah 49:34-39*
2. The sign of the yoke. *Jeremiah 27:1-11*
3. A message for King Zedekiah. *Jeremiah 27:12-22*
4. The false prophecy of Hananiah. *Jeremiah 28:1-17*
5. Concerning false and lying prophets. *Jer. 23:9-40*

A proverb: Scoffers do not like to be rebuked; they will not go to the wise. *Proverbs 15:12*

A prayer: Our hearts are heavy, O Lord, because we see so many false religions and false prophets around us. Guide us that we might give witness to the truth of the gospel and know how to respond to those who proclaim false religions.

Day 229

The shepherds of Israel and the Good Shepherd

1. The promise of a Good Shepherd. *Jeremiah 23:1-8*
2. The shepherds of Israel and the servant of David. *Ezekiel 34:1-31*
3. Jesus, the Good Shepherd. *John 10:1-21*
4. The unbelief of the Jews. *John 10:22-42*
5. The shepherd psalm. *Psalm 23:1-6*

A proverb: Do they not err that plan evil? Those who plan good find loyalty and faithfulness. *Prov. 14:22*

A prayer: O God, thank you for sending Jesus, the Good Shepherd. Thank you for this great Shepherd who helps us understand your love and your care for us. May we dwell always in your house and know your goodness. Forgive us when we have gone our own way.

Day 230

The dream of Nebuchadnezzar. The vision of Ezekiel

1. Nebuchadnezzar's dream. *Daniel 2:1-13*
2. Daniel's interpretation of the dream. *Daniel 2:14-49*
3. The vision of Ezekiel in Babylon. *Ezekiel 1:1-28*

A proverb: Those who love a pure heart and are gracious in speech will have the king as a friend. *Proverbs 22:11*

A prayer: We also praise you, Lord, for revealing deep and hidden things. Above all, we thank you for revealing the mystery of the gospel, which is for all peoples. Help us understand your revelation to us so that we might proclaim it faithfully to others.

Day 231

Jeremiah's letter. The faithfulness of Daniel's friends

1. Jeremiah's letter to the exiles. *Jeremiah 29:1-23*
2. The message to Shemaiah. *Jeremiah 29:24-32*
3. Shadrach, Meshach, and Abednego. *Daniel 3:1-30*
4. David's thanks for liberation. *Psalm 30:1-12*

A proverb: The wicked covet the proceeds of wickedness, but the root of the righteous bears fruit. *Proverbs 12:12*

A prayer: May we trust you, Lord, in what seem to be impossible situations. We thank you for those who have given their lives in faithfulness to you. Be with Christians today who are suffering persecution for your name.

Day 232

Ezekiel begins his prophetic ministry

1. God's call to Ezekiel. *Ezekiel 2:1—3:15*
2. A sentinel for the house of Israel. *Ezekiel 3:16-27*
3. The symbol of the siege of Jerusalem. *Ezek. 4:1-17*
4. Ezekiel announces the nature of Jerusalem's destruction. *Ezekiel 5:1-17*
5. Jerusalem as a useless vine. *Ezekiel 15:1-8*

A proverb: A truthful witness saves lives, but one who utters lies is a betrayer. *Proverbs 14:25*

A prayer: Help us be faithful watchers in the world in which we live. May our words be true to what you have spoken to us, exposing evil deeds and also pointing out the way to renew covenant faithfulness. Forgive us for our lack of compassion for those going toward destruction.

Day 233

Ezekiel's prophecies against Jerusalem

1. Coming destruction by sword, famine, and plague. *Ezekiel 6:1-14*
2. The coming of the end. *Ezekiel 7:1-27*
3. Ezekiel's vision of idolatry at the temple. *Ezekiel 8:1-18*
4. The idolaters will be killed. *Ezekiel 9:1-11*

A proverb: The sacrifice of the wicked is an abomination; how much more when brought with evil intent. *Proverbs 21:27*

A prayer: O Lord, forgive us for the idolatry of jealousy, putting too much value on temporary things. May we learn to be content with what we have. Teach us the joy of sharing with others and of developing friendships that can honor you.

Day 234

The promise of judgment, exile, and restoration

1. The glory of God departs from the temple. *Ezekiel 10:1-22*
2. Ezekiel symbolizes the coming exile. *Ezek. 12:1-28*
3. Judgment upon the leaders of Israel. *Ezek. 11:1-13*
4. The promise of restoration. *Ezekiel 11:14-25*

A proverb: The wicked are overthrown and are no more, but the house of the righteous will stand. *Proverbs 12:7*

A prayer: Thank you, Lord, for removing our hearts of stone and giving us hearts of flesh. Thank you for giving us a new spirit. Teach us your decrees and laws so that we may follow them and live. You are our God, and by your grace, we are your people.

Day 235

Prophecy concerning false prophets, idolatry and the kings

1. Punishment for the false prophets. *Ezekiel 13:1-23*
2. Condemnation of idolatry of the heart. *Ezekiel 14:1-11*
3. Four judgments for Jerusalem. *Ezekiel 14:12-23*
4. The parable of the two eagles. *Ezekiel 17:1-24*

A proverb: Evil plans are an abomination to the Lord, but gracious words are pure. *Proverbs 15:26*

A prayer: Forgive us for our wicked and impure thoughts, O God. May our words and thoughts honor you and be a blessing to others. Thank you for giving life to what was weak and lifeless in our past experience. We rejoice in your mercy and love, and we commit ourselves to keep your covenant.

Day 236

The unfaithfulness of Jerusalem

1. The allegory of Jerusalem as a prostitute. *Ezekiel 16:1-43*
2. Jerusalem compared to Samaria and to Sodom. *Ezekiel 16:44-52*
3. Restoration for Jerusalem. *Ezekiel 16:53-63*
4. A lament for Israel's kings. *Ezekiel 19:1-14*

A proverb: Good sense wins favor, but the way of the faithless is their ruin. *Proverbs 13:15*

A prayer: Thank you, God, for loving us and taking us as your children. Thank you for the beauty of holiness that you have given us. We want to be faithful to your love. Forgive our waywardness. We trust in your promises, today and forever.

Day 237

Punishment for the rebellion of Israel

1. The rebellion of Israel. *Ezekiel 20:1-29*
2. Judgment and restoration. *Ezekiel 20:30-44*
3. The destruction of Jerusalem by Babylon is foretold. *Ezekiel 21:1-27*

A proverb: One's own folly leads to ruin, yet the heart rages against the Lord. *Proverbs 19:3*

A prayer: Lord, forgive us when we too have been rebellious against your Word. Give us faith to put your commands into practice even though doing so may be difficult. Help us see the seriousness of our unfaithfulness. May we live as those who have turned and received your healing.

Day 238

The sins of Jerusalem and of Samaria

1. The sins of Jerusalem. *Ezekiel 22:1-31*
2. The two adulterous sisters:
   a. The sin of Oholah. *Ezekiel 23:1-10*
   b. The sin of Oholibah. *Ezekiel 23:11-21*
   c. The punishment of Oholibah. *Ezekiel 23:22-35*
   d. God's judgment on both sisters. *Ezekiel 23:36-49*

A proverb: Sheol and Abaddon lie open before the Lord, how much more human hearts! *Proverbs 15:11*

A prayer: O all-seeing God, we are greatly concerned because of the bloodshed, idolatry, and sexual perversion we see on all sides. Free us from any joy we may experience in watching or reading about these evils. May our joy be in you and in living for you.

Day 239

The siege of the city of Jerusalem
1. The siege. *2 Kings 25:1; Jeremiah 39:1; 52:4-5*
2. The parable of the cooking pot. *Ezekiel 24:1-14*
3. The death of Ezekiel's wife. *Ezekiel 24:15-27*
4. Jeremiah warns Zedekiah; the Hebrew slaves. *Jeremiah 34:1-7; 34:8-22*
5. Zedekiah inquires of the Lord. *Jeremiah 21:1-14*
6. Jeremiah's complaint. *Jeremiah 20:7-18*

A proverb: The wealth of the rich is their strong city; in their imagination it is like a high wall. *Proverbs 18:11*

A prayer: O Lord, be with us when we are disgraced because of your name. You have rescued us from doing evil. We honor your name.

Day 240

Prophecies against neighboring nations
1. Against the South (Negeb). *Ezekiel 20:45-49*
2. Against Ammon. *Ezekiel 21:28-32; 25:1-7*
3. Against Moab, Edom, and Philistia. *Ezek. 25:8-17*
4. Obadiah against Edom. *Obadiah 1:1-21*
5. Ezekiel against Edom (Mount Seir). *Ezek. 35:1-15*
6. A psalm of Asaph against the enemies of Israel. *Psalm 83:1-18*

A proverb: When wickedness comes, contempt comes also; and with dishonor comes disgrace. *Proverbs 18:3*

A prayer: Forgive us when we have taken satisfaction in the misfortune of others. Give us compassion for those who are suffering as well as for the evildoer. May your gospel be extended to them.

Day 241

The prophecies of Ezekiel against Tyre and Sidon

1. Ezekiel on the destruction of Tyre. *Ezekiel 26:1-21*
2. A lament for Tyre. *Ezekiel 27:1-36*
3. Tyre is proud and will be destroyed. *Ezekiel 28:1-19*
4. Ezekiel's prophecy against Sidon. *Ezekiel 28:20-26*

A proverb: There is a way that seems right to a person, but its end is the way to death. *Proverbs 14:12*

A prayer: Forgive us for our pride, O God, even if that pride is in the blessing you have given us. We recognize your mercy and goodness and that what we have or what we are is only because of your grace. We want to honor you in our actions and in our attitudes.

Day 242

Prophecies of Ezekiel against Egypt

1. A prophecy against Pharaoh. *Ezekiel 29:1-16*
2. Nebuchadnezzar will destroy Egypt. *Ezek. 29:17-21*
3. A lament for Egypt. *Ezekiel 30:1-19*
4. The captivity of Egypt announced. *Ezekiel 30:20-26*
5. The allegory of the cedar in Lebanon. *Ezek. 31:1-18*
6. The power of God over the nations. *Psalm 76:1-12*

A proverb: The violence of the wicked will sweep them away, because they refuse to do what is just. *Proverbs 21:7*

A prayer: We see, Lord, how violence causes more violence. Help us understand how this vicious cycle can be broken and how peace and reconciliation can begin. Teach us your way of peace and how to be peacemakers.

Day 243

A lament for Pharaoh. Jeremiah's imprisonment

1. A lament for Pharaoh. *Ezekiel 32:1-16*
2. A lament for the hordes of Egypt and other nations. *Ezekiel 32:17-32*
3. Jeremiah arrested; Zedekiah's inquiry. *Jeremiah 37:1-21*
4. God promises restoration for Israel. *Jer. 30:1-24*

A proverb: When the wicked die, their hope perishes, and the expectation of the godless comes to nothing. *Proverbs 11:7*

A prayer: Thank you, God, for not completely destroying us because of our sin. Thank you for your discipline of justice and for your great salvation through Jesus Christ. May we forgive others as you have forgiven us. Deliver us from evil. For yours is the kingdom forever.

Day 244

The restoration of Israel

1. The promise of restoration for Jerusalem. *Jeremiah 33:1-26*
2. Restoration for all the clans of Israel. *Jeremiah 31:1-26*
3. The new covenant. *Jeremiah 31:27-40*

A proverb: To do righteousness and justice is more acceptable to the Lord than sacrifice. *Proverbs 21:3*

A prayer: Thank you, God, for the new covenant that you have made with us through the blood of Jesus Christ. May this covenant always be on our minds and upon our hearts. Thank you for your forgiveness and for making us part of your people.

Day 245

Jeremiah's last prophecies before the fall

1. Jeremiah buys a field from Hanamel. *Jer. 32:1-16*
2. Jeremiah's prayer and God's response. *Jer. 32:17-44*
3. Jeremiah thrown into a cistern. *Jeremiah 38:1-13*
4. Zedekiah questions Jeremiah again. *Jer. 38:14-28*
5. Ebed-melech will be saved. *Jeremiah 39:15-18*

A proverb: The clever see danger and hide; but the simple go on, and suffer for it. *Proverbs 27:12*

A prayer: O Lord, we recognize your sovereignty over heaven and earth. Nothing is too hard for you. Work out your purpose in our lives and in the life of the church. Thank you for your great love.

Day 246

The fall of Jerusalem and Judah

1. As Jeremiah announced, Babylonians enter Jerusalem, destroy city and temple. Zedekiah captured, his sons killed in front of him, his eyes put out. Temple plundered, burned. City wall torn down. Many killed, others carried to Babylon. Only the poor left on the land. *Jeremiah 39:2-10; 52:6-30; 2 Kings 25:2-21; 2 Chronicles 36:17-21*
2. Jeremiah returns to his home. *Jeremiah 39:11-14*
3. Ezekiel's words when he receives the report. *Ezekiel 33:21-33*

A proverb: Condemnation is ready for the scoffers, and flogging for the backs of fools. *Proverbs 19:29*

A prayer: O Lord, may your Word be to us more than beautiful love songs. Help us put into practice its teachings and its truths. Let us recognize the voice of a prophet and obey what you command.

Day 247

Laments for the fallen city of Jerusalem

1. A lament of Asaph. *Psalm 79:1-13*
2. A description of the destruction of the city. *Lamentations 1:1-22*
3. The judgment of God upon Jerusalem. *Lamentations 2:1-22*

A proverb: The heart knows its own bitterness, and no stranger shares its joy. *Proverbs 14:10*

A prayer: We too have seen cities destroyed by war. O Lord, forgive the foolishness of men and women who want to dominate and kill each other. Help us see and understand your way of working in this world. May we learn to have consideration for others, and to love our neighbors as ourselves.

Day 248

Hope after judgment

1. The punishment of Zion is complete. *Lamentations 4:1-22*
2. There is hope of liberation. *Lamentations 3:1-66*
3. A prayer of an afflicted people. *Lamentations 5:1-22*

A proverb: Anxiety weighs down the human heart, but a good word cheers it up. *Proverbs 12:25*

A prayer: We lift up our heart and hands to you, O Lord. Truly we have sinned and rebelled, but you have forgiven us. We call on you each day and thank and praise you for your redemption. Open our hearts to you in praise and adoration.

Day 249

The remnant in Judah and the migration to Egypt

1. The government of Gedaliah. *2 Kings 25:22-26*
2. Jeremiah and the remnant in Judah. *Jeremiah 40:1-12*
3. Ishmael conspires against Gedaliah. *Jeremiah 40:13—41:10*
4. Johanan rescues the people from Ishmael and flees toward Egypt. *Jeremiah 41:11—42:6*
5. Jeremiah's message for Johanan. *Jeremiah 42:7-22*
6. The migration to Egypt. *Jeremiah 43:1-7*

A proverb: A fool gives full vent to anger, but the wise quietly holds it back. *Proverbs 29:11*

A prayer: Lord, forgive us when we promise to be faithful to your Word but then disobey when it conflicts with our wishes. Help us see the results of our decisions and learn from experience.

Day 250

Prophecies of the destruction of Egypt and the restoration of Israel

1. The invasion of Egypt by Nebuchadnezzar foretold. *Jeremiah 43:8-13*
2. Jeremiah prophesies disaster for the Jews in Egypt. *Jeremiah 44:1-30*
3. God will use Cyrus to restore Israel. *Isaiah 45:1-25*

A proverb: "There is no peace," says the Lord, "for the wicked." *Isaiah 48:22*

A prayer: We praise you, O God, because there is no other like you. You are the beginning and the end. Your purpose stands. So we honor you and make your greatness known.

Day 251

Jeremiah's prophecy concerning Babylon

1. A message concerning Babylon. *Jeremiah 50:1-32*
2. The fall of Babylon foretold. *Jeremiah 50:33-46*
3. God will destroy Babylon in his vengeance. *Jeremiah 51:1-35*

A proverb: Crush a fool in a mortar with a pestle along with crushed grain, but the folly will not be driven out. *Proverbs 27:22*

A prayer: O Master of the Universe, we have seen the arrogance of rulers and nations and how they have been humiliated. Forgive us for the sin of arrogance, especially when it is based on worldly power and riches. Give us a humble and contrite spirit so that we can trust in you.

Day 252

The humiliation of Nebuchadnezzar

1. Jeremiah's final prophecy concerning Babylon's fall. *Jeremiah 51:36-64*
2. Nebuchadnezzar's dream of a tree. *Daniel 4:1-18*
3. Daniel's interpretation of the dream. *Dan. 4:19-27*
4. The humiliation of Nebuchadnezzar. *Dan. 4:28-37*
5. The ballad of the Hebrews in Babylon. *Ps. 137:1-9*

A proverb: A ruler who lacks understanding is a cruel oppressor; but one who hates unjust gain will enjoy a long life. *Proverbs 28:16*

A prayer: O Lord, we thank you for rulers of nations who recognize your sovereignty and glorify your name. May they learn justice from your Word, and may they walk humbly before you. Forgive them for their pride.

Day 253

Prophecies about the restoration of Israel

1. Jehoiachin's release. *2 Kings 25:27-30; Jer. 52:31-34*
2. New life for the mountains of Israel. *Ezek. 36:1-15*
3. Restoration for the sake of God's holy name. *Ezekiel 36:16-38*
4. The vision of the valley of dry bones. *Ezek. 37:1-14*
5. Israel and Judah to be one nation. *Ezek. 37:15-28*

A proverb: My child, do not despise the Lord's discipline or be weary of his reproof, for the Lord reproves the one he loves, as a father the son in whom he delights. *Proverbs 3:11-12*

A prayer: Thank you, God, for giving life to those who were nothing more than dry bones. Give new life to your church that it may grow in your Spirit. We also thank you for uniting all peoples in one, making us one church, that you might dwell with us.

Day 254

Ezekiel's vision of a new temple

1. The gates to the temple. *Ezekiel 40:1-37*
2. Rooms for sacrifices, for the priests. *Ezek. 40:38-47*
3. The temple itself. *Ezekiel 40:48—41:26*
4. Measurements of the temple. *Ezekiel 42:15-20*

A proverb: The poor and the oppressor have this in common: the Lord gives light to the eyes of both. *Proverbs 29:13*

A prayer: We thank you, God, for the hope you give us, that out of destruction can come new life. We praise you for not abandoning your people and for giving us hope in time of despair. We put our hope in the promise of your presence.

Day 255

The sanctuary and its rules

1. Rooms for the priests. *Ezekiel 42:1-14*
2. A description of the altar and its consecration. *Ezekiel 43:13-27*
3. Regulations regarding the temple. *Ezekiel 44:1-31*
4. Instructions regarding justice, offerings, and holy days. *Ezekiel 45:9-25*

A proverb: A false balance is an abomination to the Lord, but an accurate weight is his delight. *Prov. 11:1*

A prayer: We honor you, Lord, because you are a holy God and demand holiness of your children. Forgive us for making common what should be holy before you. We dedicate ourselves to your service. May our lives be a holy sacrifice, pleasing to you.

Day 256

The division and boundaries of the land

1. The division of the inheritance. *Ezekiel 45:1-8*
2. Instructions for the offerings of the prince. *Ezekiel 46:1-24*
3. The boundaries of the land. *Ezekiel 47:13-23*
4. The division of the territory for each tribe. *Ezekiel 48:1-29*
5. The gates of the city. *Ezekiel 48:30-35*

A proverb: Better is a little with the fear of the Lord than great treasure and trouble with it. *Prov. 15:16*

A prayer: O Lord, we thank you for your presence in our midst. We also thank you for the inheritance you have given us in Christ Jesus. May we be faithful stewards of your good gifts and use our lives for your honor and glory.

Day 257

The Spirit of God in the temple. The defeat of Gog

1. The river that flows from the temple. *Ezek. 47:1-12*
2. The glory of God returns. *Ezekiel 43:1-12*
3. The invasion and defeat of Gog. *Ezekiel 38:1-23*
4. The victory of Israel over Gog. *Ezekiel 39:1-16*
5. Sacrificial feast; return from exile. *Ezekiel 39:17-29*

A proverb: The wage of the righteous leads to life, the gain of the wicked to sin. *Proverbs 10:16*

A prayer: We have received your Holy Spirit that flows from you, O God. We praise you for the life given to the church. May your Spirit fill our lives, and may we make known to all peoples the good news of your salvation.

Day 258

The redemption of Israel by the grace of God

1. The omnipotent God helps Israel. *Isa. 40:27—41:29*
2. A hymn of praise to God. *Isaiah 42:10-17*
3. The blind and the deaf. *Isaiah 42:18-25*
4. God, Israel's Creator and Redeemer. *Isaiah 43:1-13*
5. God's mercy, Israel's unfaithfulness. *Isa. 43:14-28*
6. Israel as God's servant. *Isaiah 44:1-5, 21-28*

A proverb: The righteousness of the upright saves them, but the treacherous are taken captive by their schemes. *Proverbs 11:6*

A prayer: O Lord, we thank you for your love that has redeemed us from sin. Thank you for making this love known to your people even before the earthly ministry of Jesus Christ. Thank you for choosing us and pouring out your Spirit upon us that we might make known your goodness to all.

Day 259

Prophecies concerning the Servant-king

1. The choosing of the Servant. *Isaiah 49:1-7*
2. The restoration of Israel. *Isaiah 49:8-26*
3. Israel's sin and the Servant's obedience. *Isa. 50:1-11*
4. Everlasting salvation for Zion. *Isaiah 51:1-16*
5. The restoration of Jerusalem. *Isaiah 51:17—52:15*

A proverb: When it goes well with the righteous, the city rejoices; and when the wicked perish, there is jubilation. *Proverbs 11:10*

A prayer: We thank you, Lord, for the promise of restoration. May we experience the joy of proclaiming peace and good tidings of salvation. We pray for those whom you have called to serve you and to preach the good news of salvation in Jesus Christ.

Day 260

The future glory of Jerusalem. Visions of Daniel

1. The future glory of Jerusalem. *Isaiah 54:1-17*
2. Daniel's vision of the four beasts. *Daniel 7:1-14*
3. Interpretation of the dream. *Daniel 7:15-28*
4. Daniel's vision of the ram and the goat. *Daniel 8:1-14*
5. Interpretation of the vision. *Daniel 8:15-27*

A proverb: Wisdom is as good as an inheritance, an advantage to those who see the sun. *Ecclesiastes 7:11*

A prayer: We praise you, Lord, for the wisdom of your ways and for your presence in the world. Thank you for revealing your ways in ancient history. We pray that you may also move in our times. Above all, may your greatness be recognized in all nations and at all times.

Day 261

Isaiah's prophecy of liberation. The fall of Babylon

1. The coming captivity of Babylon. *Isaiah 46:1-13*
2. The judgment of God on Babylon. *Isaiah 47:1-15*
3. The return of Israel from Babylon. *Isaiah 48:1-21*
4. The fall of Babylon in the days of king Belshazzar. *Daniel 5:1-31*

A proverb: The righteousness of the blameless keeps their ways straight, but the wicked fall by their own wickedness. *Proverbs 11:5*

A prayer: We praise you, Lord, because you have refined us and redeemed us. Thank you for teaching us what is best for us day by day and year by year. Direct us in the way we should go, and forgive us when we have been stubborn.

Day 262

Daniel in the den of lions. Daniel's prayer

1. Daniel and the den of lions. *Daniel 6:1-28*
2. Daniel's prayer. *Daniel 9:1-19*
3. The message of Gabriel. *Daniel 9:20-27*
4. A plea for restoration. *Psalm 80:1-19*

A proverb: The righteous are delivered from trouble, and the wicked get into it instead. *Proverbs 11:8*

A prayer: O Lord, we praise you because we know that you are a living God who cares about our well-being and because your dominion will never end. Thank you for your protection in time of danger and for hearing our prayers anytime and anywhere.

Day 263

The decree of Cyrus and the return from exile
1. Cyrus's proclamation. *2 Chron. 36:22-23; Ezra 1:1-4*
2. Preparation for the return trip. *Ezra 1:5-11*
3. A list of the exiles who returned. *Ezra 2:1-70*
4. The first sacrifices on the rebuilt altar. *Ezra 3:1-6*
5. Rebuilding of the temple begun. *Ezra 3:7-13*
6. A psalm of the sons of Korah. *Psalm 87:1-7*

A proverb: The king's heart is a stream of water in the hand of the Lord; he turns it wherever he will. *Proverbs 21:1*

A prayer: We thank you, Lord, for voices with which we can sing your praises. May we always honor you with our hymns and songs. Bless those who write songs and those who honor you with musical instruments. May the deaf and dumb also have joy in honoring you.

Day 264

Other lists of exiles who returned to Jerusalem
1. The list found by Nehemiah. *Nehemiah 7:5-73*
2. Genealogies of families in Jerusalem. *1 Chronicles 9:1-34*
3. The royal line after the exile. *1 Chronicles 3:17-24*

A proverb: Do not say, "Why were the former days better than these?" For it is not from wisdom that you ask this. *Ecclesiastes 7:10*

A prayer: O Lord, we thank you for our ancestors and especially for those who were faithful to you and passed on their faith to us. May we do the same for our children and grandchildren, and for all the children in the family of God.

Day 265

Difficulties in reconstructing the temple

1. Opposition of Judah's enemies. *Ezra 4:1-5, 24*
2. Haggai's call to continue the building. *Haggai 1:1-15*
3. Haggai's exhortation to Zerubbabel. *Haggai 2:1-23*
4. Building resumed; letter to Darius. *Ezra 5:1-17*
5. Darius's answer and decree. *Ezra 6:1-12*

A proverb: The Lord is far from the wicked, but he hears the prayer of the righteous. *Proverbs 15:29*

A prayer: Forgive us, Lord, for having luxury in our own homes and not helping with your church. All we have comes from you. We dedicate everything to you for the extension of your kingdom.

Day 266

Prophecies and visions of Zechariah

1. Zechariah's call to return to the Lord. *Zechariah 1:1-6*
2. The first two visions of Zechariah. *Zech. 1:7-21*
3. A man with a measuring line. *Zechariah 2:1-13*
4. The vision of Joshua the high priest. *Zech. 3:1-10*
5. The gold lampstand, two olive trees. *Zech. 4:1-14*
6. The flying scroll, four chariots. *Zechariah 5:1—6:8*
7. A crown for Joshua. *Zechariah 6:9-15*

A proverb: The discerning person looks to wisdom, but the eyes of a fool to the ends of the earth. *Proverbs 17:24*

A prayer: Lord, we praise you for your Spirit. May your messengers preach the gospel to the ends of the world. Thank you for assuring us that this happens not by might or by power but by your Spirit.

Day 267

Blessing on Jerusalem. Temple completed
1. Justice and mercy instead of fasting. *Zech. 7:1-14*
2. The Lord's promise to bless Jerusalem. *Zech. 8:1-23*
3. Judgment on Israel's enemies. *Zechariah 9:1-8*
4. The Lord will take care of Judah. *Zech. 9:10—11:3*
5. Dedication of the temple. *Ezra 6:13-22*

A proverb: For the protection of wisdom is like the protection of money, and the advantage of knowledge is that wisdom gives life to the one who possesses it. *Ecclesiastes 7:12*

A prayer: Forgive us, Lord, when our religion has only been superficial. May our fasting be from the heart. Teach us how to do justice and show mercy and compassion rather than thinking evil.

Day 268

Esther, queen of Persia, and the plot of Haman
1. Queen Vashti deposed. *Esther 1:1-22*
2. Esther made queen. *Esther 2:1-18*
3. Mordecai uncovers a conspiracy to kill king Xerxes. *Esther 2:19-23*
4. Haman's plot to kill the Jews. *Esther 3:1-15*
5. Mordecai asks Esther for help. *Esther 4:1-11*

A proverb: The one who lives alone is self-indulgent, showing contempt for all who have sound judgment. *Proverbs 18:1*

A prayer: Free us, O God, from evil people who out of pride and selfishness want to exterminate a race. We pray for those in our day who are suffering from such an evil. May we bring comfort and help to those who are suffering.

Day 269

Esther intervenes. Liberation of the Jews

1. Esther invites the king. *Esther 4:12—5:8*
2. Haman's rage against Mordecai. *Esther 5:9-14*
3. Mordecai honored by the king. *Esther 6:1-14*
4. Haman is hanged. *Esther 7:1-10*
5. The king's edict to help the Jews. *Esther 8:1-17*
6. Praise to God for his help. *Psalm 124:1-8*

A proverb: Strike a scoffer, and the simple will learn prudence; reprove the intelligent, and they will gain knowledge. *Proverbs 19:25*

A prayer: We thank you, God, for helping your people in so many situations. We praise you for your mercy and love. Teach us how we can show kindness to others even if they are our enemies. We confess our own selfishness.

Day 270

The feast of Purim. The faithfulness of God

1. The triumph of the Jews. *Esther 9:1-17*
2. The institution of the feast of Purim. *Esth. 9:18-32*
3. The greatness of Mordecai. *Esther 10:1-3*
4. The faith of the persecuted. *Hebrews 11:32-40*
5. Gratitude for the faithfulness of God. *Ps. 107:1-43*

A proverb: When the righteous triumph, there is great glory, but when the wicked prevail, people go into hiding. *Proverbs 28:12*

A prayer: We thank you, Lord, for those who have lived by faith even through suffering. We praise you that we have received an even better promise in Christ Jesus. Forgive us for our doubts and waywardness.

Day 271

Nehemiah's trip to Jerusalem

1. Nehemiah's prayer. *Nehemiah 1:1-11*
2. Artaxerxes sends Nehemiah. *Nehemiah 2:1-10*
3. Nehemiah inspects Jerusalem's walls. *Neh. 2:11-20*
4. The builders of the walls of Jerusalem. *Neh. 3:1-32*
5. A prayer of the captives. *Psalm 126:1-6*

A proverb: A desire realized is sweet to the soul, but to turn away from evil is an abomination to fools. *Proverbs 13:19*

A prayer: We put our trust in you, O God, and not in those who govern us. We praise you because you uphold the cause of the oppressed and hungry, the widow, and the fatherless. Forgive us for not doing the same. Show how we can help those in need.

Day 272

Opposition to rebuilding Jerusalem

1. The letter to Artaxerxes. *Ezra 4:6-16*
2. Artaxerxes' response. *Ezra 4:17-23*
3. The opposition of the Samaritans. *Nehemiah 4:1-23*
4. Nehemiah's abolition of usury. *Nehemiah 5:1-19*
5. The wall is completed. *Nehemiah 6:1-19*

A proverb: By the blessing of the upright a city is exalted, but it is overthrown by the mouth of the wicked. *Proverbs 11:11*

A prayer: Lord, give us the steadfastness of Nehemiah to continue serving your kingdom in spite of the opposition of the enemy. Raise up master builders among us like Nehemiah and Paul, so that we may be founded upon the true faith. May we seek and know the guidance of your Spirit.

Day 273

Ezra arrives in Jerusalem

1. Ezra's arrival in Jerusalem. *Ezra 7:1-10*
2. Artaxerxes' letter to Ezra. *Ezra 7:11-28*
3. A list of those who returned with Ezra. *Ezra 8:1-14*
4. A chronicle of the trip to Jerusalem. *Ezra 8:15-36*
5. The reading of the Law. *Nehemiah 7:73b—8:12*

A proverb: Who is like the wise man? And who knows the interpretation of a thing? Wisdom makes one's face shine, and the hardness of one's countenance is changed. *Ecclesiastes 8:1*

A prayer: We thank you for the way the Scriptures have been preserved for us. We thank you for those who have translated the Bible so we can understand it. We also give thanks for those who teach us to put its message into practice.

Day 274

The renewal of the covenant

1. Feast of tabernacles celebrated. *Nehemiah 8:13-18*
2. The Israelites confess their sins. *Nehemiah 9:1-37*
3. Covenant agreement signed. *Nehemiah 9:38—10:39*

A proverb: Those with good sense are slow to anger, and it is their glory to overlook an offense. *Proverbs 19:11*

A prayer: We thank you, O merciful God, for your patience with us and for your great salvation. We have accepted your covenant and pledged ourselves to follow you and live by the guidance of your Spirit that you have given us. May we be faithful to that covenant.

Day 275

Jerusalem residents. Dedication of the walls

1. The new city of Jerusalem. *Nehemiah 7:1-4*
2. The new settlers in Jerusalem. *Nehemiah 11:1-36*
3. The priests and Levites. *Nehemiah 12:1-26*
4. The walls of Jerusalem dedicated. *Neh. 12:27-47*
5. Tobiah's goods thrown out of the temple.
   Nehemiah 13:1-11

A proverb: What the wicked dread will come upon them, but the desire of the righteous will be granted. *Proverbs 10:24*

A prayer: We thank you, Lord, for those who lead our worship services and preach your Word. Forgive us when we have not provided for their needs as we should have done. Teach us how to give joyfully and to dedicate our talents for your church.

Day 276

The reforms of Nehemiah and Ezra

1. The reforms instituted by Nehemiah. *Neh. 13:12-31*
2. Ezra's concern and prayer regarding intermarriage. *Ezra 9:1-15*
3. The people's confession of sin. *Ezra 10:1-17*
4. A list of those guilty of intermarriage. *Ezra 10:18-44*

A proverb: The wise will inherit honor, but stubborn fools, disgrace. *Proverbs 3:35*

A prayer: Lord, we pray for those contemplating marriage, that they may find partners of similar faith. Forgive us when we have not taught the importance of marrying "in the Lord." May your presence in our marriages and in our homes give honor to you.

Day 277

The prophecy of Joel
1. The invasion of locusts. *Joel 1:1-12*
2. A call to repentance. *Joel 1:13-20*
3. The day of the Lord. *Joel 2:1-27*
4. Judgment of the nations. *Joel 3:1-21*
5. Praise for God's mighty deeds. *Psalm 66:1-20*

A proverb: When a scoffer is punished, the simple become wiser; when the wise are instructed, they increase in knowledge. *Proverbs 21:11*

A prayer: We thank you, Lord, for hearing and answering our prayers. You have not withheld your love from us. We praise and honor you. Forgive us when we have kept silent and have not made your goodness known.

Day 278

Warnings of Malachi and Isaiah against unfaithful priests
1. Israel's blemished sacrifices. *Malachi 1:1-14*
2. Malachi's admonition for the priests. *Mal. 2:1-16*
3. Words that have wearied God. *Mal. 2:17; 3:13-18*
4. "There is no peace for the wicked." *Isa. 57:14-21*
5. False and true religion. *Isaiah 58:1-12*
6. The greatness of God. *Psalm 147:1-20*

A proverb: A rebuke strikes deeper into a discerning person than a hundred blows into a fool. *Prov. 17:10*

A prayer: Forgive us, God, from wearying you with our doubts and questions. Forgive us for empty rituals not backed up with holy living. May our light shine in the darkness and our lives be like a well-watered garden.

Day 279

The confession, redemption, and glory of Zion
1. God's redemption for the sins of his people. *Isaiah 59:1-21*
2. The future glory of Zion. *Isaiah 60:1-22*
3. The restoration of Zion. *Isaiah 62:1-12*
4. The future reign of God. *Isaiah 35:1-10*
5. A cry for understanding and salvation. *Psalm 119:169-176*

A proverb: No harm happens to the righteous, but the wicked are filled with trouble. *Proverbs 12:21*

A prayer: We praise you, O God, for giving us a Savior who has called us to be your people. Let the nations see your righteousness; may all people know your salvation. We glorify your name for your great works. Help us be a light to all nations.

Day 280

Judgment, salvation, and hope
1. God's day of vengeance and redemption. *Isaiah 63:1-14*
2. A plea for mercy. *Isaiah 63:15—64:12*
3. Judgment and salvation. *Isaiah 65:1-16*
4. Judgment and hope. *Isaiah 66:1-24*

A proverb: The hope of the righteous ends in gladness, but the expectation of the wicked comes to nothing. *Proverbs 10:28*

A prayer: Give us a humble and contrite spirit, O Lord. May we tremble before your Word. May our offerings always be acceptable before you, and may our praise glorify your name. Extend peace upon your church and nourish it.

Day 281

The future of Judah and Jerusalem
1. The two shepherds. *Zechariah 11:4-17*
2. Jerusalem's enemies will be destroyed. *Zech. 12:1-9*
3. Messianic prophecies. *Zechariah 12:10—13:9*
4. The day of the coming of the Lord. *Zech. 14:1-21*
5. Praise for God's help. *Psalm 146:1-10*

A proverb: One wise person went up against a city of warriors and brought down the stronghold in which they trusted. *Proverbs 21:22*

A prayer: Thank you, Lord, for cleansing us from sin and impurity. Thank you for answering us when we call on your name. Thank you for making us your people. We proclaim you as our Lord and God.

Day 282

The vision of Daniel
1. Daniel's vision of one who looked like a man. *Daniel 10:1—11:1*
2. Two Greek kings (North, South). *Daniel 11:2-28*
3. Judah to be invaded, the temple desecrated. *Daniel 11:29-45*
4. The end times. *Daniel 12:1-13*

A proverb: When the tempest passes, the wicked are no more, but the righteous are established forever. *Proverbs 10:25*

A prayer: We pray for wisdom that we may understand your Word. Help us discern how your hand has directed in history, both ancient and modern. We put our faith in you, knowing that future history is also in your hand. Thank you for sending prophets who make known your will for the future.

Day 283

Announcements of the births of John and of Jesus
1. The prophecy of Malachi. *Malachi 4:1-6*
2. Luke's introduction. *Luke 1:1-4*
3. The angels' message to Zechariah. *Zech. 1:5-25*
4. The angels' message to Mary. *Luke 1:26-38*
5. Mary's visit to Elizabeth. *Luke 1:39-56*
6. The birth of John the Baptist. *Luke 1:57-80*
7. Joseph's dream. *Matthew 1:18-25*

A prophecy: See, the former things have come to pass, and new things I now declare; before they spring forth, I tell you of them. *Isaiah 42:9*

A prayer: We marvel at your wondrous ways, O Lord. We thank you for the knowledge of salvation and forgiveness of sins which was promised in Zechariah's song.

Day 284

The birth of Jesus and the visit of the magi
1. The prophecy of Isaiah. *Isaiah 9:1-7*
2. The birth of Jesus. *Luke 2:1-20*
3. The genealogy of Jesus. *Matthew 1:1-17*
4. Presentation of Jesus in the temple. *Luke 2:21-40*
5. The visit of the magi, wise men. *Matthew 2:1-23*

A proverb: The light of the eyes rejoices the heart, and good news refreshes the body. *Proverbs 15:30*

A prayer: We thank you, Lord, for your humble birth and your coming into so many lives. Help us to share the message of peace and salvation that you came to give all peoples.

Day 285

The ministry of John the Baptist

1. The prophecy of Isaiah. *Isaiah 40:1-11*
2. The prophecy of Malachi. *Malachi 3:1-5*
3. The boy Jesus visits Jerusalem. *Luke 2:41-52*
4. The preaching of John the Baptist. *Mark 1:1-8; Matthew 3:1-12; Luke 3:1-20; John 1:19-28*
5. Jesus, the Lamb of God. *John 1:29-34*

A proverb: The ear that heeds wholesome admonition will lodge among the wise. *Proverbs 15:31*

A prayer: Forgive us, Lord, when our lives have not produced fruit in keeping with our professed faith in you. Help us live and work in such a way that others can see you in us.

Day 286

Jesus' preparation for ministry

1. A messianic psalm. *Psalm 2:1-12*
2. The baptism and temptation of Jesus. *Mark 1:9-13; Matthew 3:13—4:11; Luke 3:21-22; 4:1-13*
3. The genealogy of Jesus. *Luke 3:23-38*
4. The first disciples and the wedding in Cana. *John 1:35—2:12*

A proverb: Better to be poor and walk in integrity than to be crooked in one's ways even though rich. *Proverbs 28:6*

A prayer: Thank you, Lord Jesus, for identifying with us in your baptism and in your temptations. May we follow your example in withstanding the evil one. Help us be victorious over our temptations so you can use us in your service.

Day 287

Jesus' early ministry in Judea and Samaria

1. Cleansing the temple at Passover time. *John 2:13-25*
2. Jesus talks with Nicodemus. *John 3:1-21*
3. John's testimony about Jesus. *John 3:22-36*
4. Jesus and the Samaritan woman. *John 4:1-42*
5. Praise for the salvation of God. *Psalm 98:1-9*

A beatitude of Jesus: Blessed are those who hunger and thirst for righteousness, for they will be filled. *Matthew 5:6*

A prayer: O God, thank you for new life in Christ Jesus, new light in our lives. We who believe have been born from above, born of the Spirit. Thank you for the living water that has satisfied our thirst. May we worship in spirit and truth.

Day 288

Jesus begins his ministry in Galilee

1. The prophecy of Isaiah. *Isaiah 61:1-11*
2. Jesus rejected in Nazareth. *Luke 4:14-30*
3. Jesus heals an official's son. *John 4:43-54*
4. Jesus preaches in Galilee, calls his first disciples, speaks in the synagogue of Capernaum. *Mark 1:14-28; Matthew 4:12-22; Luke 4:31-37; 5:1-11*

A beatitude of Jesus: Blessed are the meek, for they will inherit the earth. *Matthew 5:5*

A prayer: Lord, forgive us for rejecting those in our own midst who are calling us to faithfulness. Give us faith to leave things as necessary so we can follow you in accord with your call. Make us fishers of men and women, both young and old.

Day 289

Jesus' preaching-healing ministry in Galilee

1. In Capernaum, Jesus casts out evil spirits, heals Simon's mother-in-law, travels throughout Galilee preaching and healing many people, calls Levi to follow him. *Mark 1:29-2:17; Luke 4:38-44; 5:12-32; Matthew 4:23-25; 8:1-4, 14-17; 9:1-13*

A proverb: Do not plan harm against your neighbor who lives trustingly beside you. *Proverbs 3:29*

A prayer: We thank you, Lord, for the power of your Spirit, giving health to body, mind, and soul. Your Spirit is greater than the power of evil forces around us. Thank you for the new beginning the Spirit brought through the ministry of Jesus.

Day 290

The opposition of the Pharisees

1. Jesus questioned about fasting. *Matthew 9:14-17; Mark 2:18-22; Luke 5:33-39*
2. Jesus questioned about the Sabbath. *Mark 2:23-3:6; Luke 6:1-11*
3. The healing at the pool of Beth-zatha. *John 5:1-15*
4. Jesus' response to the Jews. *John 5:16-47*

A proverb: All deeds are right in the sight of the doer, but the Lord weighs the heart. *Proverbs 21:2*

A prayer: O God, teach us how to fast and to honor you on the Lord's day. Forgive us for letting tradition hold us back when the Lord is showing us how to meet human needs. Help us find meaning for all of life so we can honor the Son of God, do good, and be prepared for the resurrection of life.

Day 291

Jesus names and teaches his disciples

1. The Song of the Servant. *Isaiah 42:1-8*
2. God's chosen Servant. *Matthew 12:14-21*
3. The fame of Jesus. *Mark 3:7-12; Luke 6:17-19*
4. The twelve disciples named. *Matthew 10:1-4; Mark 3:13-19; Luke 6:12-16*
5. Jesus teaches his disciples. *Luke 6:20-49; Matthew 5:1-3; 7:1-5, 21-29*
6. Jesus and the Law. *Matthew 5:17-20; Luke 16:16-17*

A beatitude of Jesus: Blessed are the peacemakers, for they will be called children of God. *Matthew 5:9*

A prayer: Teach us, O Lord, to love our enemies and be true peacemakers. Forgive us for judging others. Help us see ourselves as others see us.

Day 292

Jesus' healing and teaching ministry continues

1. Jesus heals a centurion's servant, raises a widow's son, answers John's disciples, forgives a sinful woman in Simon's house. *Luke 7:1-8:3*
2. Parallel accounts. *Matthew 8:5-13; 11:1-19*
3. Jesus possessed by Beelzebub? *Mark 3:20-30*

A proverb: One who spares words is knowledge-able; one who is cool in spirit has understanding. *Proverbs 17:27*

A prayer: We praise you, Lord, for your power and authority to heal. Even more, we praise you for your power to forgive sins. Give us faith that we might find in you healing for body and soul. Thank you for the mighty ministry of Jesus in rescuing us from bondage to Satan.

Day 293

Jesus' teaching through parables

1. Jesus explains the kingdom of God, his use of parables. *Mark 4:1-29; Luke 8:4-18; Matthew 13:1-30, 36-43*
2. A psalm of David. *Psalm 131:1-3*

A proverb: Anyone who tills the land will have plenty of bread, but one who follows worthless pursuits will have plenty of poverty. *Proverbs 28:19*

A prayer: Thank you, Lord Jesus, for the wisdom of your teachings. Help us sow the word with faithfulness. Thank you for the abundant fruit you have given in lives and ministry. Our hope is in you.

Day 294

Parables. Lord's Prayer. Tempest calmed

1. More parables. *Mark 4:30-34; Luke 13:18-21; Matthew 13:31-35, 44-53*
2. Jesus' teaching on prayer and fasting. *Matthew 6:1-18; 7:7-11; Luke 11:1-13*
3. The concern of Jesus' family. *Mark 3:31-35; Luke 8:19-21; Matthew 12:46-50*
4. Jesus calms the tempest. *Mark 4:35-41; Luke 8:22-25; Matthew 8:23-27*

A proverb: From the fruit of the mouth one is filled with good things, and manual labor has its reward. *Proverbs 12:14*

A prayer: Lord, forgive us for doing acts of righteousness to be seen of others. Teach us how to give, to pray, and to fast so that we may minister to those in need and know your presence in our lives. Thank you for doing great things with small seeds.

Day 295

Three miracles of Jesus

1. Jesus crosses the Sea of Galilee, casts a demon out of a man of Gerasene, returns, heals a woman who touches his garment, and raises a dead girl. *Mark 5:1-43; Luke 8:26-56; Matthew 8:28-34; 9:18-26*

A proverb: Hope deferred makes the heart sick, but a desire fulfilled is a tree of life. *Proverbs 13:12*

A prayer: We praise you, Lord Jesus, for your power to cast out demons, raise the dead, and heal the suffering. We put our faith in you. Give us power and gifts to overcome the forces of evil. We pray for those who have gifts of healing and deliverance.

Day 296

Jesus ends his ministry in Galilee

1. Jesus heals the blind and mute. *Matthew 9:27-38*
2. Rejected in Nazareth. *Matt. 13:54-58; Mark 6:1-6*
3. The mission of the twelve. *Matthew 10:5-16; Mark 6:7-13; Luke 9:1-6*
4. Jesus announces persecution. *Matthew 10:17-25*
5. The death of John the Baptist. *Matthew 14:1-12; Mark 6:14-29; Luke 9:7-9*
6. Praise in the midst of persecution. *Ps. 119:161-168*

A proverb: Do not be wise in your own eyes; fear the Lord, and turn away from evil. It will be a healing for your flesh and a refreshment for your body. *Proverbs 3:7-8*

A prayer: Thank you, Lord, for working through our suffering for your name. Help us be faithful to you in whatever place or situation we may be. Deliver persecuted Christians from harm.

Day 297

The feeding of the 5000. Jesus walks on the water

1. The prophecy of Zephaniah. *Zephaniah 3:14-20*
2. The people follow Jesus to the desert to hear his teaching. He feeds them with five loaves and two fishes. That night Jesus walks on the water to join his disciples returning by boat. *Matthew 14:13-36; Mark 6:30-56; Luke 9:10-17; John 6:1-24*

A proverb: The simple believe everything, but the clever consider their steps. *Proverbs 14:15*

A prayer: We thank you, Lord Jesus, for your compassion on those who are hungry for your word. Help us share our loaves and fishes that they might know your truth and your power. Forgive us for doubting your word. Since you are with us, we are not afraid.

Day 298

The Jews reject Jesus

1. Jesus, the bread of life. *John 6:25-66*
2. Jesus and the traditions of the Jews. *Matthew 15:10-20; Mark 7:1-19*
3. Thanksgiving for the salvation of God. *Ps. 116:1-19*

A proverb: Just as water reflects the face, so one human heart reflects another. *Proverbs 27:19*

A prayer: We thank you, Lord Jesus, for being the bread of life and feeding us with true nourishment. We thank you, O God, for sending Jesus into the world to give his life so that we might have life. Help us understand all that this means, and help us share this truth with others. We offer you a thanksgiving sacrifice for your wonderful salvation.

Day 299

Jesus' trip to Tyre and then to Decapolis

1. Jesus goes to Tyre with his disciples, and casts a demon out of a little girl; goes to the Decapolis, heals a man deaf and mute, and feeds 4000 people; crosses to Magadan, meets the Pharisees. *Matthew 15:21—16:12; Mark 7:24—8:26*
2. Jesus and the adulteress woman. *John 7:53—8:11*
3. The righteous and the wicked. *Psalm 1:1-6*

A proverb: A fool takes no pleasure in understanding, but only in expressing personal opinion. *Proverbs 18:2*

A prayer: Lord, forgive us for being judgmental toward sinful people. We thank you for your love that forgives sins. Teach us how to confront sinners and at the same time be ready to forgive.

Day 300

Jesus in Caesarea Philippi

1. Jesus goes north of Galilee to region of Caesarea Philippi. Peter confesses that Jesus is the Christ, the Son of God. Jesus foretells his coming death. Jesus climbs a mountain (Hermon?) and is transfigured. *Matthew 16:13—17:13; Mark 8:27—9:13; Luke 9:18-36; John 6:67-71*
2. A messianic psalm of David. *Psalm 110:1-7*

A proverb: The human spirit is the lamp of the Lord, searching every innermost part. *Proverbs 20:27*

A prayer: We too believe that you, Jesus, are the Christ, the Son of God. You laid down your life that we might live. Guide us with your Spirit that we may take the cross and follow you.

Day 301

Jesus casts out an evil spirit and returns to Capernaum

1. Jesus comes down the mountain, casts an evil spirit out of a boy, what the disciples could not do. Again he talks with his disciples about his coming death and about humility and following him. *Luke 9:37-62; Mark 9:14-50; Matthew 17:14— 18:9; 8:18-22*

A proverb: When pride comes, then comes disgrace; but wisdom is with the humble. *Proverbs 11:2*

A prayer: Lord, forgive us for our pride, for vying with each other for honors or authority. Teach us true humility, to be servants of our Lord. Forgive us for causing others to sin. May our lives honor your name and tell of your love.

Day 302

Jesus in Jerusalem at the Feast of Tabernacles

1. Jesus teaches in the temple. *John 7:1-24*
2. The Pharisees fail to arrest Jesus. *John 7:25-52*
3. Jesus continues his teaching in Jerusalem. *John 8:12-30*
4. The claims of Jesus about himself. *John 8:31-59*

A proverb: The tongue of the righteous is choice silver; the mind of the wicked is of little worth. *Proverbs 10:20*

A prayer: We praise you, Lord, because you are eternal and were sent from God with the truth. We are of this world, but you have given us eternal life. We believe in your word and in your salvation. Help us share these treasures with others.

Day 303

The healing of a blind man. The seventy

1. The soul who sins will die. "Repent and live."
   Ezekiel 18:1-32
2. The healing of a man born blind. *John 9:1-41*
3. The seventy sent out. *Luke 10:1-20; Matt. 11:20-24*

A proverb: A bad messenger brings trouble, but a
faithful envoy, healing. *Proverbs 13:17*

A prayer: O Lord, we see the consequences of sin in
the world, and we recognize that we are responsible for our own acts. We rejoice that our names are
written in heaven; we also rejoice when we see
your power over evil. We pray that there may be
many faithful workers in your kingdom.

Day 304

On the way to Jerusalem, Jesus teaches

1. The word from the mouth of God. *Isaiah 55:10-13*
2. Jesus teaching and healing on his way to Jerusalem. Hypocrisy of Pharisees. He visits the home
   of Mary and Martha. *Luke 10:21-24, 38-42;
   11:14-36; 12:1-12*
3. Some parallel accounts. *Matthew 10:26-33;
   11:25-30; 12:22-45*

A promise: Ho, everyone who thirsts, come to the
waters; and you that have no money, come, buy
and eat! Come, buy wine and milk without money
and without price. *Isaiah 55:1*

A prayer: O God, we thank you for enlightening
our lives. Give us courage not to fear those who can
only destroy our bodies. Keep us from blaspheming
your Holy Spirit.

Day 305

More teachings of Jesus, especially in Luke
1. The parable of watchful servants. *Luke 12:35-48*
2. Jesus brings division. *Luke 12:49-59; Matthew 10:34-42*
3. The need for repentance. *Luke 13:1-9*
4. The narrow door. *Luke 13:22-30*
5. Jesus' sorrow over Jerusalem. *Luke 13:31-35*
6. Jesus in the house of a Pharisee. *Luke 14:1-14*
7. The cost of being a disciple. *Luke 14:25-35*

A proverb: In all your ways acknowledge him, and he will make straight your paths. *Proverbs 3:6*

A prayer: O Lord, help us count the cost of following you. Forgive us if we have taken that decision lightly. Show us what we should leave behind.

Day 306

More parables of Jesus, set in his ministry, especially in Luke
1. The great banquet. *Luke 14:15-24*
2. The lost sheep. *Luke 15:1-7; Matthew 18:10-14*
3. The lost coin. *Luke 15:8-10*
4. The lost son. *Luke 15:11-32*
5. The shrewd manager. *Luke 16:1-15*
6. The rich man and Lazarus. *Luke 16:19-31*
7. The persistent widow. *Luke 18:1-8*
8. The Pharisee and the tax collector. Luke 18:9-14

A proverb: Like a bird that strays from its nest is one who strays from home. *Proverbs 27:8*

A prayer: Thank you, Lord, for your love seeking and accepting us in spite of our sin. May we have the same love toward those who stray from you.

Day 307

Jesus' ministry in Perea

1. Jesus' teaching regarding divorce. *Mark 10:1-12; Luke 16:18*
2. On restoration of a member. *Matthew 18:15-22*
3. On forgiveness. *Matthew 18:23-35*
4. Forgiveness, faith, and service. *Luke 17:1-10*
5. The healing of the ten lepers. *Luke 17:11-19*
6. The coming of the kingdom of God. *Luke 17:20-37*
7. Jesus blesses the children. *Luke 18:15-17; Mark 10:13-16; Matthew 19:13-15*
8. The blessing of forgiveness. *Psalm 32:1-11*

A beatitude of Jesus: Blessed are the merciful, for they will receive mercy. *Matthew 5:7*

A prayer: O Lord, we have been blessed with your forgiveness. May we learn how to forgive others and how to restore church members who fall into sin. Teach us to receive your kingdom like a child.

Day 308

Jesus on his way to Jerusalem

1. A rich man asks Jesus about eternal life. Jesus again announces his death. James and John make a request. Jesus heals a blind man. *Mark 10:17-52; Matthew 19:16-30; 20:17-34; Luke 18:18-43*

A proverb: The rich is wise in self-esteem, but an intelligent poor person sees through the pose. *Proverbs 28:11*

A prayer: Forgive us, Lord, when our riches keep us from full participation in your kingdom. Teach us how to use your gifts of possessions for your honor and glory. Help us to be faithful managers.

Day 309

Jesus and Zacchaeus. Jesus raises Lazarus

1. Jesus and Zacchaeus. *Luke 19:1-10*
2. The parable of the pounds. *Luke 19:11-27*
3. The raising of Lazarus. *John 11:1-44*
4. The plot to kill Jesus. *John 11:45-57*
5. The plot to kill Lazarus. *John 12:9-11*
6. The blessings of fearing the Lord. *Psalm 112:1-10*

A proverb: Wealth is a ransom for a person's life, but the poor get no threats. *Proverbs 13:8*

A prayer: Lord, teach us how to be generous and how to be good stewards of all you have given us. May we understand what it means to fear you. Help us believe that in Jesus we have life eternal.

Day 310

Jesus' entrance in Jerusalem

1. Jesus enters Jerusalem on a colt to the shouts of crowds. He curses a fig tree without figs, then enters the temple and clears it of buying and selling. Some Greeks ask to see Jesus. *Matthew 21:1-22; Mark 11:1-26; Luke 19:28-48; John 12:12-26*
2. The king of glory. *Psalm 24:1-10*

A prophecy: Rejoice greatly, O daughter Zion! Shout aloud, O daughter Jerusalem! Lo, your king comes to you; triumphant and victorious is he, humble and riding on a donkey, on a colt, the foal of a donkey. *Zechariah 9:9*

A prayer: We put our faith in you, O Lord. Forgive us for our doubts. Teach us to pray in faith, believing that your reign is growing. May our churches be houses of prayer for those of all nations.

Day 311

Jesus' response to questions of Jewish leaders

1. Jewish leaders question Jesus on his authority to lead. He responds with a question they cannot answer, then tells several parables directed at the leaders. Pharisees try to trick Jesus with a question about paying taxes. *Mark 11:27—12:17; Luke 20:1-26; Matt. 21:23—22:22 (two extra parables)*

A proverb: It is honorable to refrain from strife, but every fool is quick to quarrel. *Proverbs 20:3*

A prayer: Lord, we want to give you all that belongs to you. Help us give to our government what is demanded without going against your call for peacemaking and doing right. We owe our whole lives to you.

Day 312

Jesus' continued confrontation with Jewish leaders

1. Sadducees question Jesus about the resurrection. A Pharisee asks about the greatest commandment. Jesus asks them about the identification of the Christ. He also observes the offering of a widow. *Mark 12:18-44; Luke 20:27—21:4; Matthew 22:23-33, 41-46*
2. Other teachings of Jesus. *John 12:27-50*

A proverb: To make an apt answer is a joy to anyone, and a word in season, how good it is! *Proverbs 15:23*

A prayer: We praise you because you are a God of the living. We want to love you with all our heart and love our neighbors. Forgive us for self-love that puts others down. Help us to love the glory that comes from God rather than human glory.

Day 313

Against Pharisees; about Jerusalem

1. Jesus criticizes Pharisees. *Matthew 23:1-15, 23-36; Luke 11:37-54*
2. Prophecy about Jerusalem. *Matthew 23:37—24:2; Mark 13:1-2; Luke 21:5-6*
3. The judgment of the nations. *Matthew 25:31-46*
4. The workers in the vineyard. *Matthew 20:1-16*

A proverb: Do not envy the violent and do not choose any of their ways; for the perverse are an abomination to the Lord, but the upright are in his confidence. *Proverbs 3:31-32*

A prayer: Keep us from hypocrisy and pretense. Help us practice what we preach. May we serve you by serving others, feeding the hungry, giving drink to the thirsty, clothing the naked, and visiting those sick or in prison. Forgive us for our desire to destroy evildoers. May we be as generous as you are.

Day 314

About coming events and the end of the age

1. Signs of the destruction of Jerusalem and the end of the age. *Matt. 24:3-28; Mark 13:3-23; Luke 21:7-24*
2. The parable of the ten bridesmaids. *Matt. 25:1-13*
3. The parable of the talents. *Matthew 25:14-30*

A proverb: Wealth hastily gotten will dwindle, but those who gather little by little will increase it. *Proverbs 13:11*

A prayer: Come, Lord Jesus! Teach us how to watch and understand the signs. May we encourage each other in faithfulness. We look for God's victory over sin and the fullness of God's kingdom.

Day 315

Jesus' teaching on the eve of the Passover

1. The coming of the Son of Man. *Matthew 24:29-51; Mark 13:24-37; Luke 21:25-38*
2. Leaders plot to kill Jesus; Judas agrees to hand Jesus over to them. In Bethany, Jesus is anointed by a woman. *Matthew 26:1-16; Mark 14:1-11; Luke 22:1-6; John 12:1-8*

A proverb: The righteous gives good advice to friends, but the way of the wicked leads astray *Proverbs 12:26*

A prayer: We know, Lord, that your words will not pass away. You will come again, but we do not know the time. Help us be prepared and watching.

Day 316

The Passover supper of Jesus with his disciples

1. The preparations. *Mark 14:12-16; Luke 22:7-13*
2. Jesus washes the feet of his disciples. *John 13:1-20*
3. The meal. *Mark 14:17-26; Luke 22:14-23*
4. Paul repeats the instructions. *1 Cor. 11:17-34*
5. The dispute of the disciples. *Luke 22:24-30*
6. Jesus announces his betrayal. *John 13:21-30*
7. The new commandment: Love! *John 13:31-35*

A proverb: Those who are generous are blessed, for they share their bread with the poor. *Proverbs 22:9*

A prayer: Thank you, Lord, for these signs, these symbols: sharing the bread and the cup and washing feet. They remind us of what you did for us and bind us together in faith and hope. Forgive us when they have only been empty forms. Teach us to love one another and humbly to serve each other.

Day 317

Jesus' final teachings and his prayer for his disciples

1. The promise of the Holy Spirit. *John 14:15-31*
2. The vine and the branches. *John 15:1-11*
3. The rejection of the world. *John 15:18—16:4*
4. The work of the Holy Spirit. *John 16:5-15*
5. Grief will turn to joy. *John 16:16-33*
6. Jesus prays for his disciples. *John 17:1-26*

A proverb: Whoever pursues righteousness and kindness will find life and honor. *Proverbs 21:21*

A prayer: Thank you for your love, O Lord. May our lives be united in you to bear fruit. Thank you for the promise of the Holy Spirit; may the Spirit work freely in our lives. Bind us together in love so that the world may know, believe, and obey you.

Day 318

Jesus in the garden of Gethsemane

1. Jesus foretells that Peter will deny him, goes out with his disciples to the garden, and prays in agony to his Father. Judas comes with soldiers and police, who arrest Jesus. *Matthew 26:30-56; Mark 14:27-52; Luke 22:31-53; John 13:36-38; 18:1-11*

A proverb: Well meant are the wounds a friend inflicts, but profuse are the kisses of an enemy. *Proverbs 27:6*

A prayer: We thank you, Lord Jesus, for your suffering on our behalf. We take from you the best example for faithfulness in doing the will of God, even at the cost of life itself. Forgive us when we have not been willing to stand up for you.

Day 319

Jesus tried before Sanhedrin, other rulers

1. Jesus taken to Annas, then to Caiaphas. The Sanhedrin questions Jesus. Peter disowns Jesus. Jesus is beaten, sent to Pilate, then to Herod. Herod questions Jesus, sends him to Pilate. Judas hangs himself. *John 18:12-27; Mark 14:53-72; Matthew 26:57—27:10; Luke 22:54—23:12*

A proverb: Truthful lips endure forever, but a lying tongue lasts only a moment. *Proverbs 12:19*

A prayer: Forgive us, Lord Jesus, when we have denied your name before others. Help us witness courageously of your love, your salvation, and your presence in our lives. May others learn to know you through our witness.

Day 320

Jesus tried before Pilate and sentenced to death

1. Pilate questions Jesus, does not find a crime worthy of death. He offers to release Jesus or a rebel leader. The crowd asks for Barabbas. Pilate agrees and washes his hands. Soldiers mock Jesus and crucify him. *Mark 15:1-24; Luke 23:13-34; Matthew 27:11-36; John 18:28—19:18*

A proverb: Do not quarrel with anyone without cause, when no harm has been done to you. *Proverbs 3:30*

A prayer: We confess you, Jesus of Nazareth, as our king. Forgive us when we live as though someone else were our master. Help us see your heavenly reign in this world and what that means for us in daily life.

Day 321

The crucifixion and death of Jesus

1. Jesus, King of the Jews, crucified at 9:00 a.m., a robber on each side. People insult Jesus; soldiers divide his clothing. Jesus speaks to God, to the robbers, to his mother, and to John, then dies. It becomes dark; the veil of the temple is torn. Soldiers pierce Jesus' side. *Matthew 27:37-56; Mark 15:25-41; Luke 23:35-49; John 19:19-37*
2. The suffering of the Messiah. *Isaiah 53:1-12a*

A prophecy: Yet he bore the sin of many, and made intercession for the transgressors. *Isaiah 53:12b*

A prayer: O Lord, we confess that, like sheep, we have gone astray. Our hearts are full of gratitude for your great love. We confess our sins and treasure your pardon and your gift of eternal life.

Day 322

The burial and resurrection of Jesus

1. Joseph puts Jesus' body in a tomb. Three women come, find the stone rolled away. Two angels say Jesus has risen. They tell the disciples; Peter and John come to see. Jesus appears to Mary Magdalene, then to a couple on the road. *Matt. 27:57—28:15; Mark 15:42—16:13; Luke 23:50—24:35; John 19:38—20:18*

A proverb: The fear of the Lord is a fountain of life, so that one may avoid the snares of death. *Proverbs 14:27*

A prayer: Lord, your power to raise Jesus is wonderful. Thank you for new life from Jesus and victory over sin through the power of the Spirit.

Day 323

Jesus appears to the disciples. The ascension
1. Jesus appears. *Luke 24:36-48; John 20:19-31*
2. Appearances to four in Galilee. *John 21:1-25*
3. Jesus commissions the apostles. *Luke 24:49; Mark 16:14-18; Matthew 28:16-20*
4. Ascension. *Mark 16:19-20; Luke 24:50-53; Acts 1:6-11*
5. Matthias chosen to replace Judas. *Acts 1:12-26*
6. Praise in the temple. *Psalm 134:1-3*

A proverb: The lot is cast into the lap, but the decision is the Lord's alone. *Proverbs 16:33*

A prayer: Thank you, Lord, for those who have gone to all nations, preaching, baptizing, and teaching. May you give them the power of your Spirit to confront evil and teach your commandments.

Day 324

Pentecost and the primitive church
1. The introduction of Acts. *Acts 1:1-5*
2. The coming of the Holy Spirit. *Acts 2:1-13*
3. Peter's first sermon. *Acts 2:14-41*
4. The prophecy of Joel. *Joel 2:28-32*
5. The fellowship of the new church. *Acts 2:42-47*
6. A crippled beggar healed; Peter's discourse. *Acts 3:1-10, 11-26*

A prophecy: Let the wicked forsake their way, and the unrighteous their thoughts; let them return to the Lord, that he may have mercy on them, and to our God, for he will abundantly pardon. *Isaiah 55:7*

A prayer: We praise you, Lord, for the coming of the Holy Spirit into our lives. Help us understand what this means. Come, Holy Spirit, come!

Day 325

Trials and victories of the early church

1. The arrest of Peter and John. *Acts 4:1-22*
2. Life and worship in the early church. *Acts 4:23-37*
3. Ananias and Sapphira. *Acts 5:1-11*
4. Signs and wonders of the apostles. *Acts 5:12-16*
5. The arrest of the apostles. *Acts 5:17-42*
6. The choosing of the seven. *Acts 6:1-7*

A proverb: The good obtain favor from the Lord, but those who devise evil he condemns. *Prov. 12:2*

A prayer: We praise you, Lord, for the power of the Holy Spirit as manifested in the early church and also today. Give us power to speak your Word without fear and to recognize those to whom you have granted gifts of preaching, teaching, and service.

Day 326

The persecution and extension of the early church

1. The arrest of Stephen. *Acts 6:8-15*
2. Stephen's defense. *Acts 7:1-53*
3. The stoning of Stephen. *Acts 7:54-60*
4. The persecution of the Jerusalem church. *Acts 8:1-3*
5. Preaching in Samaria. *Acts 8:4-25*

A proverb: To impose a fine on the innocent is not right, or to flog the noble for their integrity. *Proverbs 17:26*

A prayer: Thank you, Lord, for those willing to give their lives for the preaching of your Word. Give us assurance and power even when our lives are not in danger. Be with churches suffering persecution today.

Day 327

The ministry of Philip and of Peter
1. Philip and the Ethiopian. *Acts 8:26-40*
2. Peter in Lydda and Joppa. *Acts 9:32-43*
3. Peter and Cornelius. *Acts 10:1-48*
4. Peter's report to the church in Jerusalem. *Acts 11:1-18*

A prophecy: Seek the Lord while he may be found, call upon him while he is near. *Isaiah 55:6*

A prayer: We praise you for your plan to proclaim the gospel to all peoples. May it truly be a gospel of peace that can break down racial barriers. Forgive us for our discriminatory attitudes and actions.

Day 328

The conversion of Saul. The church in Antioch
1. The conversion of Saul. *Acts 9:1-19*
2. Saul in Damascus and Jerusalem. *Acts 9:20-31*
3. The church in Antioch. *Acts 11:19-30*
4. Peter's miraculous escape from prison. *Acts 12:1-19*
5. Herod's death. *Acts 12:20-25*
6. The appointing of the first missionaries. *Acts 13:1-3*
7. The Lord is light and salvation. *Psalm 27:1-14*

A proverb: No one who conceals transgressions will prosper, but one who confesses and forsakes them will obtain mercy. *Proverbs 28:13*

A prayer: Lord, we thank you for women and men who have been called by your Spirit to minister in the church in different ways, according to their gifts. We pray that the church may have discernment to know your will and to recognize the gifts you have given. May we not quench the Spirit.

Day 329

The first missionary trip

1. A prophecy of Isaiah. *Isaiah 55:2-5*
2. Paul and Barnabas in Cyprus. *Acts 13:4-12*
3. Paul's sermon in Pisidian Antioch. *Acts 13:13-52*
4. Iconium, Lystra, and Derbe. *Acts 14:1-20*
5. The return to Antioch in Syria. *Acts 14:21-28*

A proverb: The fruit of the righteous is a tree of life, but violence takes lives away. *Proverbs 11:30*

A prayer: O Lord, fill us with joy and with the Holy Spirit when others scoff at your Word. Let us know your power and your presence. Guide the leaders of the church that they may see the importance of disciplining and encouraging new believers.

Day 330

Council in Jerusalem. Second missionary journey

1. Decision of the Jerusalem council. *Acts 15:1-21*
2. The letter to the Gentile believers. *Acts 15:22-35*
3. Paul and Silas are joined by Timothy. *Acts 15:36—16:5*
4. Paul's vision and Lydia's conversion. *Acts 16:6-15*
5. Paul and Silas imprisoned in Philippi. *Acts 16:16-40*
6. A psalm of praise. *Psalm 111:1-10*

A proverb: The way of the guilty is crooked, but the conduct of the pure is right. *Proverbs 21:8*

A prayer: Thank you, Lord, for giving church leaders discernment when believers disagree about biblical interpretation or other matters. May we all be open to the leading of your Spirit.

Day 331

Paul's letter to the Galatians

1. An introduction. *Galatians 1:1-10*
2. Paul's apostolic authority. *Galatians 1:11—2:10*
3. Paul opposes Peter. *Galatians 2:11-21*
4. The Spirit is received by faith. *Galatians 3:1-18*
5. The purpose of the Law. *Galatians 3:19—4:7*
6. God is our refuge and strength. *Psalm 46:1-11*

A proverb: Treasures gained by wickedness do not profit, but righteousness delivers from death. *Proverbs 10:2*

A prayer: Forgive us, Lord, for trusting in rules. Thank you for redemption in Christ, based on faith. Help us understand the purpose of God's Law.

Day 332

Paul's exhortation to the Galatians

1. Slavery of the Law. *Galatians 4:8-31*
2. The freedom of Christ. *Galatians 5:1-15*
3. The gifts of the Spirit. *Galatians 5:16-26*
4. Doing good for all. *Galatians 6:1-18*
5. God's revelation through Creation and by his Word. *Psalm 19:1-14*
6. The faithfulness of the Lord. *Psalm 99:1-9*

A teaching of Jesus: Enter through the narrow gate; for the gate is wide and the road is easy that leads to destruction, and there are many who take it. For the gate is narrow and the road is hard that leads to life, and there are few who find it. *Matthew 7:13-14*

A prayer: Lord, forgive us for acts opposed to the Spirit. Produce in us the fruit and works of the Spirit. May we carry one another's burdens.

Day 333

Paul in Thessalonica, Berea, Athens, and Corinth

1. Paul in Thessalonica and Berea. *Acts 17:1-15*
2. Paul in Athens. *Acts 17:16-34*
3. Paul in Corinth. *Acts 18:1-17*
4. Paul's first letter to the Thessalonians.
   1 Thessalonians 1:1-10
5. Paul's ministry in Thessalonica. *1 Thessalonians 2:1-16*
6. An exhortation to praise God. *Psalm 67:1-7*

A proverb: Scoffers set a city aflame, but the wise turn away wrath. *Proverbs 29:8*

A prayer: We thank you, Lord, for believers who have made the message of the gospel ring out to those around them. May we have faith, love, and endurance to give witness to your salvation.

Day 334

Paul's exhortations to the Thessalonians

1. Timothy's mission. *1 Thessalonians 2:17—3:13*
2. Lives that please God. *1 Thessalonians 4:1-12*
3. Various instructions. *1 Thessalonians 5:12-28*
4. Sinners will be punished. *2 Thessalonians 1:1-12*
5. The man of lawlessness. *2 Thessalonians 2:1-12*
6. Closing exhortations. *2 Thessalonians 2:13—3:18*

A proverb: The name of the Lord is a strong tower; the righteous run into it and are safe. *Proverbs 18:10*

A prayer: Forgive us, Lord, for idleness, but keep us from being busybodies. May our lives be sanctified by your Spirit so that we may share in the glory of Jesus Christ. Help us stand firm in the teaching we have received through your Word.

Day 335

From Corinth to Antioch and then to Ephesus

1. The responsibility of the watcher, a sentinel.
   Ezekiel 33:1-20
2. Priscilla, Aquila, and Apollos. *Acts 18:18-28*
3. Paul in Ephesus. *Acts 19:1-22*
4. The riot in Ephesus. *Acts 19:23-41*
5. A prayer in midst of danger. *Psalm 120:1-7*

A proverb: If the wise go to law with fools, there is ranting and ridicule without relief. *Proverbs 29:9*

A prayer: We praise you, God, for your justice to those who have repented of their sins and turned to you. May we be encouraged to be faithful sentinels, warning the wicked to turn from their ways, and giving a witness of your love and salvation.

Day 336

Paul's writing to Corinthians from Ephesus

1. The problem of division in the church.
   1 Corinthians 1:1-17
2. The wisdom of God. *1 Corinthians 1:18-31*
3. Wisdom comes from the Spirit. *1 Cor. 2:1-16*
4. Our only foundation is Jesus Christ. *1 Cor. 3:1-23*
5. Paul's authority. *1 Corinthians 4:1-21*

A proverb: The fear of the Lord is instruction in wisdom, and humility goes before honor. *Proverbs 15:33*

A prayer: Forgive us, Lord, for our divisions. Help us find unity in the one foundation that is Jesus Christ. Forgive us for depending on human wisdom and not seeking the wisdom that comes from your Spirit. May we be trustworthy stewards of the mysteries of God.

Day 337

On Christian liberty, self-discipline

1. The rights of an apostle. *1 Corinthians 9:1-27*
2. Warnings from Israel's history. *1 Cor. 10:1-22*
3. On self-discipline. *1 Corinthians 10:23—11:1*
4. Propriety in worship. *1 Corinthians 11:2-16*
5. The importance of God's Word. *Psalm 119:25-32*

A proverb: Do not forsake your friend or the friend of your parent; do not go to the house of your kindred in the day of your calamity. Better is a neighbor who is nearby than kindred who are far away. *Proverbs 27:10*

A prayer: Lord, help us take into account the good of others. May we discipline ourselves to help others draw near to you and to your love.

Day 338

Spiritual gifts

1. The nature of spiritual gifts. *1 Corinthians 12:1-11*
2. One body with many parts. *1 Corinthians 12:12-31*
3. The preeminence of love. *1 Corinthians 13:1-13*
4. The gifts of prophecy and tongues. *1 Cor. 14:1-25*
5. Orderly worship. *1 Corinthians 14:26-40*
6. Unity among kindred. *Psalm 133:1-3*

A proverb: Do not let loyalty and faithfulness forsake you; bind them around your neck, write them on the tablet of your heart. So you will find favor and good repute in the sight of God and of people. *Proverbs 3:3-4*

A prayer: Thank you, Lord, for the spiritual gifts you distribute in the church. Help us use them for your glory and with love.

Day 339

The resurrection of the dead
1. The resurrection of Christ. *1 Corinthians 15:1-11*
2. The resurrection of the dead. *1 Cor. 15:12-34*
3. The resurrected body. *1 Corinthians 15:35-58*
4. Various personal requests. *1 Corinthians 16:1-24*
5. Jesus comforts his disciples. *John 14:1-14*

A beatitude of Jesus: Blessed are those who mourn, for they will be comforted. *Matthew 5:4*

A prayer: We praise you, Lord, for the promise of eternal life and for the spiritual bodies we will receive after death. Thank you for victory over sin and death through Jesus Christ and for the consolation this gives us. Thus may we be steadfast in the work of the Lord.

Day 340

More messages to Corinth from Paul, likely in Macedonia
1. Paul journeys to Macedonia. *Acts 20:1*
2. An introduction. *2 Corinthians 1:1-11*
3. A change in Paul's plans. *2 Corinthians 1:12—2:11*
4. Ministers of a new covenant. *2 Cor. 2:12—3:18*
5. Treasures in jars of clay. *2 Corinthians 4:1-18*
6. Our heavenly dwelling. *2 Corinthians 5:1-10*

A proverb: Better is open rebuke than hidden love. *Proverbs 27:5*

A prayer: We long to be in your presence, O Lord. Thank you for the Holy Spirit given to us as a guarantee of what is to come in the future life. We do not lose heart, even when we are afflicted. May we so live by faith that we can honor you in all things.

Day 341

Ministry of reconciliation. An offering

1. Ambassadors for Christ. *2 Corinthians 5:11—6:2*
2. Paul's trials and hardships. *2 Corinthians 6:3-13*
3. The unequal yoke. *2 Corinthians 6:14—7:1*
4. Paul's joy. *2 Corinthians 7:2-16*
5. Generous giving for the saints. *2 Cor. 8:1—9:15*

A proverb: Some give freely, yet grow all the richer; others withhold what is due, and only suffer want. *Proverbs 11:24*

A prayer: It is your love, O God, that compels us no longer to live for ourselves. May we give generously of our lives and our possessions so that others may be reconciled with you and have their needs supplied. Forgive us for our selfishness.

Day 342

Paul defends his ministry

1. Paul begins his defense. *2 Corinthians 10:1-18*
2. Paul and the false apostles. *2 Corinthians 11:1-15*
3. Paul boasts about his sufferings. *2 Cor. 11:16-33*
4. Paul's vision and his thorn in the flesh.
   2 Corinthians 12:1-13
5. Paul to visit Corinth. *2 Corinthians 12:11—13:10*
6. Final greetings. *2 Corinthians 13:11-14*

A proverb: Blows that wound cleanse away evil; beatings make clean the innermost parts. *Prov. 20:30*

A prayer: O Lord, forgive us for boasting of personal accomplishments. May we rejoice only in what you have done in our lives. Help us recognize the authority of leaders in the church. Grant them continued wisdom.

Day 343

Paul writes to the Romans, from Corinth
1. Paul journeys to Corinth. *Acts 20:2*
2. Paul's plans to visit Rome. *Romans 1:1-17*
3. God's righteous judgment. *Romans 2:1-16*
4. The Jews and the Law. *Romans 2:17-3:8*
5. No one is righteous. *Romans 3:9-20*
6. Righteousness through faith. *Romans 3:21-31*
7. The results of justification. *Romans 5:1-21*

A proverb: Who can say, "I have made my heart clean; I am pure from my sin"? *Proverbs 20:9*

A prayer: With our whole hearts, O God, we thank you for justifying us through the faith of Jesus Christ. May we have that same faith, and may your grace reign through righteousness to bring eternal life through Christ.

Day 344

Dead to sin and alive through the Spirit
1. Dead to sin and alive in Christ. *Romans 6:1-14*
2. Slaves to righteousness. *Romans 6:15-23*
3. An analogy taken from marriage. *Romans 7:1-6*
4. The struggle with sin. *Romans 7:7-25*
5. Life through the Spirit. *Romans 8:1-27*
6. More than conquerors. *Romans 8:28-39*

A proverb: By loyalty and faithfulness iniquity is atoned for, and by the fear of the Lord one avoids evil. *Proverbs 16:6*

A prayer: O Lord, we confess our struggle with sin, but we praise you that through Jesus Christ we are not condemned. May the law of the Spirit reign in our lives so we can be more than conquerors.

Day 345

Israel and the plan of God

1. God's election of Israel. *Romans 9:1-27*
2. Israel's unbelief; justification by faith. *Romans 9:30—10:21*
3. The remnant of Israel. *Romans 11:1-10*
4. Salvation for the Gentiles. *Romans 11:11-24*
5. The salvation of all Israel. *Romans 11:25-36*

A prophecy: For my thoughts are not your thoughts, nor are your ways my ways, says the Lord. *Isa. 55:8*

A prayer: We praise you, Lord, for the depth of your wisdom and your judgments. Thank you for your mercy that has brought salvation to all peoples. Forgive us for our unbelief. Open our hearts to the truths of your salvation for all humankind.

Day 346

Exhortations for Christians

1. A living sacrifice and a life of love. *Rom. 12:1-21*
2. Being subject to governing authorities. *Rom. 13:1-7*
3. The practice of love. *Romans 13:8-14*
4. Concern for those of weak faith. *Rom. 14:1—15:13*
5. Paul plans to visit Rome. *Romans 15:14-33*

A teaching of Jesus: In everything do to others as you would have them do to you; for this is the law and the prophets. *Matthew 7:12*

A prayer: Lord, forgive us for thinking more of ourselves than we should. May our love for one another be sincere. Keep us from being a stumbling block to fellow believers. Help us overcome evil with good. Teach us what it means to obey God first of all and to be subject to our governments.

Day 347

Conclusion of Paul's third missionary journey
1. Paul's personal greetings. *Romans 16:1-27*
2. Trip from Greece to Miletus. *Acts 20:3-16*
3. Paul's farewell message in Miletus. *Acts 20:17-38*
4. The trip to Jerusalem. *Acts 21:1-16*
5. Those who trust in the Lord. *Psalm 125:1-5*

A prophecy: For as the heavens are higher than the earth, so are my ways higher than your ways and my thoughts than your thoughts. *Isaiah 55:9*

A prayer: We thank you, Lord, that the message of salvation is for both Jews and Greeks. We pray for those who are sharing the gospel today with both Jews and Arabs. Give them wisdom so that the gospel can break down walls of hatred.

Day 348

Paul's defense and his transfer to Caesarea
1. Paul's arrest in the temple. *Acts 21:17—22:2*
2. Paul tells of his conversion and call. *Acts 22:3-29*
3. Paul before the Sanhedrin. *Acts 22:30—23:11*
4. The plot to kill Paul. *Acts 23:12-22*
5. Paul's transfer to Caesarea. *Acts 23:23-35*

A proverb: Deceit is in the mind of those who plan evil, but those who counsel peace have joy. *Proverbs 12:20*

A prayer: O Lord, we thank you for men and women who have been called to give testimony about you and have done so faithfully in spite of adverse circumstances. We pray for those who are doing so today. May your presence be with them and protect them from violence.

Day 349

Paul's greetings. Defense before Festus, Agrippa

1. Paul's trial before Felix. *Acts 24:1-26*
2. Paul's defense before Festus and his appeal to Caesar. *Acts 24:27—25:12*
3. Festus consults King Agrippa. *Acts 25:13-22*
4. Paul's defense before Agrippa and Bernice. *Acts 25:23—26:32*

A proverb: Inspired decisions are on the lips of a king; his mouth does not sin in judgment. *Prov. 16:10*

A prayer: We thank you, Lord, for those over the centuries who have testified before kings and governors and called them to true belief. Guide us in finding ways to testify of your will for all people as well as your will for the church of Christ.

Day 350

Paul's journey from Caesarea to Rome

1. The beginning of the journey. *Acts 27:1-12*
2. The storm on the sea. *Acts 27:13-26*
3. The shipwreck. *Acts 27:27-44*
4. The stay on the isle of Malta. *Acts 28:1-10*
5. Paul's arrival and stay in Rome. *Acts 28:11-31*
6. God is King of all the earth. *Psalm 47:1-10*

A proverb: The clever do all things intelligently, but the fool displays folly. *Proverbs 13:16*

A prayer: We greatly exalt you, Lord God, because you are King of all nations. Thank you for calling us to follow you and be your people. We praise you for the way you worked in the life of Paul and the lives of many others who have gone to nations far and near to preach your gospel of salvation.

Day 351

Paul's letter to the Colossians
1. Thanksgiving and prayer. *Colossians 1:1-14*
2. Christ and the church. *Colossians 1:15-2:5*
3. The dangers of deceptive philosophies. *Col. 2:6-23*
4. Rules for a life of holy living. *Colossians 3:1—4:6*
5. Greetings and conclusion. *Colossians 4:7-18*

A proverb: Fools think their own way is right, but the wise listen to advice. *Proverbs 12:15*

A prayer: Forgive us, Lord, when we continue to submit to the rules of this world rather than the rules of Christ. Take from us anger, rage, malice, slander, lies, and filthy language. Set our minds upon things above.

Day 352

Paul's letter to the Philippians
1. Thanksgiving and prayer. *Philippians 1:1-11*
2. Paul's chains advance the gospel. *Phil. 1:12-30*
3. Taking on the attitude of Christ. *Philippians 2:1-18*
4. Timothy and Epaphroditus. *Philippians 2:19-30*
5. Pressing on toward the goal. *Philippians 3:1-21*
6. Final exhortations and greetings. *Phil. 4:2-23*

An exhortation: Therefore, my brothers and sisters, whom I love and long for, my joy and crown, stand firm in the Lord in this way, my beloved. *Philippians 4:1*

A prayer: Help us, Lord, find purpose and joy in our lives, even during hardships. We pray for those who need to live with physical handicaps, that they may find joy in you as well as ways to make their lives an honor for you.

Day 353

Paul's first letter to Timothy

1. A warning against false teachers. *1 Timothy 1:1-11*
2. Personal testimony, exhortation. *1 Timothy 1:12-20*
3. Instructions for worship. *1 Timothy 2:1-15*
4. Instructions for bishops (overseers) and deacons. *1 Timothy 3:1-16*
5. Instructions for Timothy. *1 Timothy 4:1-16*
6. Advice on widows, elders, slaves; final charge. *1 Timothy 5:1—6:2; 6:20-21*

A proverb: Perfume and incense make the heart glad, but the soul is torn by trouble. *Proverbs 27:9*

A prayer: Lord of the church, we pray that you will guide and bless leaders in the church. Forgive us for criticizing them behind their backs. Help us support those you have called.

Day 354

Paul's second letter to Timothy

1. Personal encouragement. *2 Timothy 1:1—2:13*
2. Exhortation to sound doctrine. *2 Tim. 2:14—3:9*
3. Paul's charge to Timothy. *2 Timothy 3:10—4:8*
4. Teachings from Paul's first letter. *1 Timothy 6:3-19*
5. The conclusion of the second letter. *2 Tim. 4:9-22*

A proverb from Jesus: Do not give what is holy to dogs; and do not throw your pearls before swine, or they will trample them under foot and turn and maul you. *Matthew 7:6*

A prayer: Thank you, Lord, for your inspired Word, making us wise unto salvation. May we learn from it regularly for rebuke, correction, and training in righteousness. Equip us for every good work.

Day 355

Peter writes about a life of holiness
1. Thanksgiving for a living hope. *1 Peter 1:1-12*
2. Exhortation to holiness. *1 Peter 1:13—2:3*
3. The Living Stone and a chosen people. *1 Peter 2:4-12*
4. Exhortations to submission. *1 Peter 2:13—3:7*
5. Exhortations to godly living. *1 Peter 3:8—4:11*

A beatitude of Jesus: Blessed are the pure in heart, for they will see God. *Matthew 5:8*

A prayer: Thank you, God, for making us a chosen people and a royal priesthood. May we be living stones, built on the foundation of Christ Jesus. May our living be holy as you are holy. Teach us how to live in harmony with each other.

Day 356

The danger of false doctrine
1. True knowledge. *2 Peter 1:1-21*
2. False prophets and teachers. *2 Peter 2:1-22*
3. Warnings against false teachers. *Jude 1:1-23*
4. False prophets. *Matthew 7:15-20*
5. Instructions for elders. *1 Peter 5:1-14*

A proverb: The words of the mouth are deep waters; the fountain of wisdom is a gushing stream. *Proverbs 18:4*

A prayer: O Lord, may the power of the Holy Spirit help us stand firm in our faith in spite of suffering and in the midst of so many false teachings around us. Teach us humility before each other and before you.

Day 357

Teachings from John's first epistle

1. Jesus Christ is our defense. *1 John 2:1-17*
2. The love of God. *1 John 3:1-10*
3. Love in God's family. *1 John 3:11-24*
4. God's love and ours. *1 John 4:1-21*
5. Various teachings. *1 John 5:1-21*

A proverb: Hatred stirs up strife, but love covers all offenses. *Proverbs 10:12*

A prayer: We praise you, Lord, for your great love extended to us even before we knew you. May we live in that love and learn how to love each other as you have loved us. May our love for others point them to your love.

Day 358

Letters from James and John

1. Trials and temptations. *James 1:1-18*
2. Pure religion. *James 1:19-27*
3. True faith. *James 2:14-26*
4. A definition of faith. *Hebrews 11:1-2*
5. Friendship with the world. *James 4:1-10*
6. Patient suffering and prayer. *James 5:7-11, 13-20*
7. John's second epistle. *2 John 1:1-13*
8. The example of Gaius. *3 John 1:1-15*

A proverb: The righteous know the rights of the poor; the wicked have no such understanding. *Proverbs 29:7*

A prayer: Forgive us, Lord, for being only listeners. May we put into practice your teachings so that our faith can be strong in times of suffering. Thank you for those who have faithfully prayed and taught us.

Day 359

On persecution, Christ's second coming
1. Being salt and light in the world. *Matthew 5:11-16*
2. God disciplines his children. *Hebrews 12:1-17*
3. Suffering for being a Christian. *1 Peter 4:12-19*
4. Warning against antichrists. *1 John 2:18-29*
5. The coming of the Lord. *1 Thessalonians 4:13—5:11; 2 Peter 3:1-18*

A beatitude of Jesus: Blessed are those who are persecuted for righteousness' sake, for theirs is the kingdom of heaven. *Matthew 5:10*

A prayer: Lord, may we be true salt and light in the world. We accept the discipline of suffering, knowing that you care for us. May we grow in grace.

Day 360

The apostle John's visions and letters
1. Prologue, greetings, vision of the exalted Christ. *Revelation 1:1-20*
2. The letter to the church at Ephesus. *Rev. 2:1-7*
3. To the church at Smyrna. *Revelation 2:8-11*
4. To the church at Pergamum. *Revelation 2:12-17*
5. To the church at Thyatira. *Revelation 2:18-29*
6. To the church at Sardis. *Revelation 3:1-6*
7. To the church at Philadelphia. *Revelation 3:7-13*
8. To the church at Laodicea. *Revelation 3:14-22*
9. A vision of the throne in heaven. *Revelation 4:1-11*

A proverb: The crucible is for silver, and the furnace is for gold, but the Lord tests the heart. *Prov. 17:3*

A prayer: Forgive our lukewarmness, O God. Make us aware of what our wealth does to our faith. Refine us and clothe us with your Spirit's power.

Day 361

The seven seals and the six trumpets

1. The scroll and the Lamb. *Revelation 5:1-14*
2. The first six seals. *Revelation 6:1-17*
3. The great multitude in white robes. *Rev. 7:1-17*
4. The seventh seal. *Revelation 8:1-5*
5. The first six trumpets. *Revelation 8:6—9:21*

A proverb: There is severe discipline for one who forsakes the way, but one who hates a rebuke will die. *Proverbs 15:10*

A prayer: We thank you, God, that with the blood of the slain Lamb, Jesus Christ, we have been redeemed and have become a kingdom of priests to serve you. Thank you for those who have suffered martyrdom for the faith.

Day 362

The seventh trumpet and the six figures

1. The angel and the little scroll. *Revelation 10:1-11*
2. The two witnesses. *Revelation 11:1-14*
3. The seventh trumpet. *Revelation 11:15-19*
4. The woman and the dragon. *Revelation 12:1-17*
5. The two beasts. *Revelation 13:1-18*
6. The Lamb and the three angels. *Revelation 14:1-13*

A proverb: When calamity comes, the wicked are brought down, but even in death the righteous have a refuge. *Proverbs 14:32, NIV*

A prayer: We praise you, God, for the promise that those who die in the Lord are blessed, for the new song you have put in our mouths, and for the gospel being proclaimed to every nation, tribe, language and people. Thank you for victory over Satan.

Day 363

The judgment of God and the fall of Babylon
1. The judgment of God. *Revelation 14:14-20*
2. The seven angels with seven plagues. *Rev. 15:1-8*
3. The seven bowls of God's wrath. *Rev. 16:1-21*
4. The woman and the beast. *Revelation 17:1-18*
5. The fall of Babylon. *Revelation 18:1-24*

A proverb: The evil bow down before the good, the wicked at the gates of the righteous. *Proverbs 14:19*

A prayer: O Lord, your wrath destroyed the wealth, power, and greatness of Rome and other nations. Save us from deception by worldly powers and from taking part in their ungodly actions. We praise you because you are just and true.

Day 364

Wedding supper. The New Jerusalem
1. The wedding supper of the Lamb. *Rev. 19:1-10*
2. The Rider on the white horse. *Revelation 19:11-21*
3. The thousand years and the day of judgment. *Revelation 20:1-15*
4. The new Jerusalem. *Revelation 21:1-27*
5. The river of life. *Revelation 22:1-5*
6. New heavens and a new earth. *Isaiah 65:17-25*
7. The Lord is our watch. *Psalm 121:1-8*

A proverb: All the days of the poor are hard, but a cheerful heart has a continual feast. *Proverbs 15:15*

A prayer: Lord, we trust you to bring the world to fulfillment. We praise you for the promise you give us of a new heaven and a new earth and for the wonder of eternal life in your presence. We know your Word is trustworthy and true.

Day 365

God has spoken to us

1. The Word has become flesh. *John 1:1-18*
2. The Word of life. *1 John 1:1-10*
3. God has spoken to us. *Hebrews 1:1—2:4*
4. Words that are trustworthy and true. *Revelation 22:6-21*
5. The Word of God is right and true. *Psalm 33:1-22*
6. A doxology. *Jude 1:24-25*

A proverb: Pleasant words are like a honeycomb, sweetness to the soul and health to the body. *Proverbs 16:24*

A prayer: We thank you, God, for your Word. It is trustworthy and true. Even more, we praise you for the Word that became flesh in Jesus Christ. We await his second coming. To the only God our Savior be glory, majesty, power, and authority, through Jesus Christ our Lord. Amen.

Index

Bɪʙʟɪᴄᴀʟ texts in canonical order, with the day when read.

26:63
27:12-14

The Author

Fᴿᴏᴍ twenty-one years of age, Delbert Erb has served with the Mennonite Board of Missions and the Argentina Mennonite Church. He went to Argentina as an administrator, became a pastor, and then moved into teaching. From 1984 to 1995 he was in charge of the Mennonite program for theological education in the congregation and taught in the Buenos Aires Bible Institute. In the 1960s he also managed a chicken hatchery.

Delbert was born in Kansas, studied at Hesston (Kansas) College and Goshen (Indiana) College. During several extended leaves from Argentina, he finished his master of divinity degree at Associated Mennonite Biblical Seminary, Elkhart, Indiana. His first wife, Ruth Landis, died of cancer in 1982. They have three children: David and Miguel in Buenos Aires, and Patricia Erb Delfin in Cochabamba, Bolivia.

Erb is now retired in the city of Choele Choel in Argentina with his wife, Frieda Schellenberg. They do some teaching in the local Mennonite congregation, where they are members, and help with the mission effort of the Mennonite Church. In 1987 Delbert published a book in Guatemala, *Bienaventurados los Pacificadores* (Blessed are the peacemakers).

Joy — (Ps 30:5, 11; 33:21;
97:11; 132:16; PR 29)

From God (Ec 2:26; Ro 15:13),
In the Lord (Ps 9:2; 104:34
Isa 9:3; 29:19; 41:16; 61:10;
Lu 1:47; Rom 5:11),
In Christ (Php 3:3; 4:4;
1 Pe 1:8).
In the word of God
(Ps 19:8; 119:14, 16, 111, 162
Jer 15:16),
In worship (2Ch 7:10;
EZR 6:22; Ne 12:43.